ROB NOLASCO

WRITING

UPPER – INTERMEDIATE

KT-444-062

OXFORD SUPPLEMENTARY SKILLS

SERIES EDITOR: ALAN MALEY

OXFORD UNIVERSITY PRESS
1987

Oxford University Press
Walton Street, Oxford OX2 6DP

Oxford New York Toronto
Delhi Bombay Calcutta Madras Karachi
Petaling Jaya Singapore Hong Kong Tokyo
Nairobi Dar es Salaam Cape Town
Melbourne Auckland

and associated companies in
Beirut Berlin Ibadan Nicosia

Oxford is a trade mark of Oxford University Press

ISBN 0 19 453406 5

© Oxford University Press 1987

Set by Promenade Graphics Ltd, Cheltenham

Printed in Hong Kong

Illustrations by:
Rupert Besley   David Haldane   Peter Joyce   Gerald Rose

The publishers would like to thank the following for permission to
reproduce photographs:

J Allan Cash Ltd; Barnaby's Picture Library; Catharine Blackie;
Central Office of Information; Colorsport; Format
Photographers; The Hutchison Library; Network Photographers;
Rex Features; Brian and Sal Shuel; Spectrum Colour Library;
Alex Dufort/Sunday Times; Victoria and Albert Museum.

Acknowledgements

Acknowledgements are made to the following writers and
publishers who have allowed us to use material that falls within
their copyright:

A Ashley and Oxford University Press for ideas from *A
Handbook of Commercial Correspondence* (1984); Brian Bethell
and Viking Books for an extract from *The Defence Diaries of
W Morgan Petty* (page 63); Jon Blundell and Oxford University
Press for an extract from *English Visa 3* (1985) (page 2); Peter
Brent and George Weidenfeld and Nicolson Ltd for an extract
from *Far Arabia* (page 63); Company (September 1986) for an
extract from a short story competition (page 1); the Consumers'
Association for an extract from the *Handy Household Tips*
booklet (page 24/25); Cosmopolitan for the article about public
conveniences (August 1986) (page 48) and for material about
animal rights (October 1986) (page 47); C Downing and Oxford
University Press for an extract from *Tales of the Hodja* (1964)
(page 19); Robert A Dutch and Longman Group UK for an
extract from *Roget's Thesaurus* (page 30); Family Circle for the
Pasta and Tomato Sauce recipe (July 1986) (page 29) and the
letter entitled *Memory Man* (August 1986) (page 18); General
Accident Fire and Life Assurance Corporation p.l.c. for an
extract from a motor accident report form (page 72); Graham
Greene and The Bodley Head Ltd for an extract from *In Search of
a Character* (page 63/64); The Guardian (16 August 1986) for an
extract from the article *Postmen deliver headache to DA* (page
79); Harper and Row Publishers Inc. for a quote by Charles Lamb
from *The Public Speaker's Treasure Chest* (page 14); The Health
Education Authority for extracts from *Safety in the home* (page 8)
and *Play it safe!* (page 24/25); Harold G Henderson and Charles E
Tuttle Co., Inc., of Tokyo, Japan for haiku from *Haiku In English*
(page 68); Adrian Henri and Deborah Rogers Ltd for extracts
from Adrian Henri's *Autobiography* (page 66/67); Her Majesty's
Stationery Office and the Department of Transport and the
Central Office of Information for an extract from *Do's and Don'ts*
(page 24/25); Laurie Lee and The Hogarth Press for an extract
from *A Rose for Winter* (page 57); Roger Lewis and John Inglis
and the National Extension College for extracts from *Report
Writing* (page 6); The Local Government Training Board for an
extract from a LGTB publication (page 3); The Observer for an
extract from *Paradise Lost* (page 46/47); Colin Peacock and
Croom Helm Ltd for an extract from *Teaching Writing* (page 9);
Punch (20 August 1986) for extracts of newspaper and magazine
mistakes (page 80/81); The Reader's Digest Association Ltd for
extracts from *What To Do In An Emergency* (pages 8 and 24/25);
Brian Shuel and Webb and Bower (Publishers) Ltd for an extract
from the *National Trust Guide to Traditional Customs of Britain*
(page 22); Sony (UK) Ltd for an extract from the Sony Video 8
brochure (page 26); H A Swan and Oxford University Press for
an extract from the *Oxford Preliminary Exam Book* (1983) (page
1); Times Newspapers Ltd for an extract from an article in The
Times (16 July 1986) entitled *Surgeons caught in jobs queue* (page
43); University of Cambridge Local Examinations Syndicate for
composition material and formats from the First Certificate in
English examination; University of Oxford Delegacy of Local
Examinations for material from EFL exams (page 82/83).

While the publishers have made every effort to trace copyright
holders of material, we have not been able to clear permission in
every case.

CONTENTS

FOREWORD

This series covers the four skill areas of Listening, Speaking, Reading and Writing at four levels — elementary, intermediate, upper-intermediate and advanced. Although we have decided to retain the traditional division of language use into the 'four skills', the skills are not treated in total isolation. In any given book the skill being dealt with serves as the *focus* of attention and is always interwoven with and supported by other skills. This enables teachers to concentrate on skills development without losing touch with the more complex reality of language use.

Our authors have had in common the following principles, that material should be:

- creative — both through author-creativity leading to interesting materials, and through their capacity to provoke creative responses from students;
- interesting — both for their cognitive and affective content, and for the activities required of the learners;
- fluency-focused — bringing in accuracy work only in so far as it is necessary to the completion of an activity;
- task-based — rather than engaging in closed exercise activities, to use tasks with pay-offs for the learners;
- problem-solving focused — so as to engage students in cognitive effort and thus provoke meaningful interaction;
- humanistic — in the sense that the materials speak to and interrelate with the learners as real people and engage them in interaction grounded in their own experience;
- learning-centred — by ensuring that the materials promote learning and help students to develop their own strategies for learning. This is in opposition to the view that a pre-determined content is taught and identically internalized by all students. In our materials we do not expect input to equal intake.

By ensuring continuing consultation between and among authors at different levels, and by piloting the materials, the levels have been established on a pragmatic basis. The fact that the authors, between them, share a wide and varied body of experience has made this possible without losing sight of the need to pitch materials and tasks at an attainable level while still allowing for the spice of challenge.

There are three main ways in which these materials can be used:

- as a supplement to a core course book;
- as self-learning material. Most of the books can be used on an individual basis with a minimum of teacher guidance, though the interactive element is thereby lost.
- as modular course material. A teacher might, for instance, combine intermediate *Listening* and *Speaking* books with upper-intermediate *Reading* and elementary *Writing* with a class which had a good passive knowledge of English but which needed a basic grounding in writing skills.   *(Alan Maley, Madras 1987)*

INTRODUCTION TO THE TEACHER

Aims of the material

The aim of this book is to provide task-based writing practice for adult students of English at upper-intermediate level. At this level we assume that students are approaching functional competence. This means that grammatical control is adequate, and while there may still be many errors, they usually do not cause serious problems in understanding. The main areas for development are organization, register, style and tone. This book therefore concentrates on giving students practice in these aspects of the writing process through a series of relevant and motivating tasks.

Although the book was not written with any examination in mind, it provides practice for exam classes at upper-intermediate level and covers the types of writing required by examinations like the University of Cambridge First Certificate in English, in a fresh and original way.

The book can function as supplementary material or as a full-blown course in writing skills.

The approach of this book

In order to do anything successfully we need practice. At this level students want to be able to express themselves freely. However, 'free' practice can be hit and miss and students need guidance and support. This book aims to integrate attention to the writing process with guidance and support. The approach is as follows.

The book has ten units

Unit 1 Before you write is an introductory unit. It introduces students to what they need in order to become effective writers. In doing so it also introduces them to the book.

Unit 10 Getting it right is there to help students develop the ability to edit their own work.

Although there is a great deal of variety of tasks to maintain motivation and deal with the different types of writing, all the units follow a similar pattern.

- Each unit opens with a section that introduces students to the area of writing focused on in that unit.
- This is followed by sections which sensitize students to the appropriate criteria for good writing. The sections may consist of a mixture of hints and advice, checklists, questionnaires, discovery tasks and analysis of model texts.
- Where appropriate students are given practice in the subskills involved through controlled tasks (e.g., pages 53 to 57), which lead up to 'free' activities (e.g., pages 58 to 60).
- There is also a continual attempt to help students correct themselves through the use of feedback tasks, (e.g., Task 2 page 59).

The main purpose of the tasks in each unit is to help students produce acceptable versions of the type of writing the unit focuses on, but the tasks also sensitize students to aspects of the writing process which may be important elsewhere. If possible try to follow the order in the book. Teachers who intend to use most of the material should cover Unit 1 first. Unit 10 can be consulted at any time and can be used independently of the book. The checklists such as the ones on pages 12 and 34 can also be used with other material. A key is available on page 85 for some of the exercises.

How to use the material

Study the material carefully and make sure that you are familiar with the demands of each task. The timing of the tasks varies and the material is very flexible so develop a feel for what your students can cover in each lesson. Little additional preparation is needed but some classes may need more help at phrase or sentence level so plan this in. Students could also do some of the tasks as homework as guidance is built in.

   The material can be used in a variety of ways but it is ideally suited for pair and small group work in which students get the opportunity to work together.

   If you decide to use pair and group work monitor it carefully to see that it is proceeding smoothly. Provide on-the-spot correction and advice as appropriate. Although a lot of self-evaluation has been built in, students will want you to give feedback on what they have written. Ideally all the written work should be collected in and assessed. Do this after the students have tried to correct it themselves. This will help students to develop the ability to correct themselves while cutting down on your work. Try to collect a sample of work each time so that you can plan in the extra support they might need.

In correcting work you should
1   introduce a correction code with symbols for the different types of error: e.g., **sp** for spelling, **p** for punctuation, **voc** for vocabulary, etc. This encourages students to correct their own errors or ask questions to put them right.
2   let students know how successful they have been in achieving the aims of the task by including a short overall comment.
3   praise students for making an effort so that they are prepared to take risks and extend their competence.

Always build in a short period of time for students to look through corrected work.

Some additional ideas for feedback include
• getting students to report back in plenary sessions. If overhead projectors are available some of the pairs and groups could write on transparencies which could then be the focal point for discussion.

- photocopying 'model' student work for display on a class notice-board.
- getting groups to routinely exchange work.

Make sure that students understand the value of
- thinking through what they are going to write. This should include planning (e.g., jotting down a list of points), as well as thinking about what is required of them (i.e., the criteria for success in the type of writing they are attempting).
- checking what they have written carefully.

One way of achieving this would be to discuss the approach of this book.

1 Introduction

The aim of this unit is to introduce you to this book. In doing so it should help you assess your strengths and weaknesses as a writer.

Task 1

Look at the following samples of writing tasks. Some of them are from EFL coursebooks and exams. Others are from outside the EFL classroom. Look at them carefully and number each task on a scale from one to five. One indicates that you would find the task almost impossible to attempt, and five that you would find it quite easy.

Sample 1

Sample 2
A popular teacher is leaving your school. Write the speech you would make at the farewell party. (Between 120 and 180 words)

Sample 3
Write a descriptive account of a visit to a crowded beach. (About 350 words)

Sample 4
This short story competition appeared in *Company*, a magazine for women.

1 Write 1000 words on two of the following subjects:
   • My local hero.
   • Reasons to be cheerful.
   • When Prince Charming turns into a frog.

2 Write the first paragraph to a novel entitled *The Singing Typist*.

Sample 5

You were cycling to the Royal School of English when you saw an accident. These pictures describe what you saw. Compare them with the report that Tony Sharp, the driver of the red sports car, gave to the police.

Report on Accident

1 I was driving very slowly towards the traffic lights. They had just changed from red to green so I didn't stop. I was signalling to turn right at the crossroads.

2 I had just turned right – there was nothing coming towards me – when a man ran into the road in front of me. He hadn't waited for the lights to change – they were still green for me and red for him.

3 I missed him, but by then the lights had changed and a green car had knocked him over. The driver didn't see him.

4 I stopped, and after I had checked that the man was all right I drove home. I didn't phone the police because it wasn't my fault.
Tony Sharp

Now write *your* report.
1 *I was cycling to the Royal School of English when a red sports car passed me. It was going very _____ .*

Sample 6

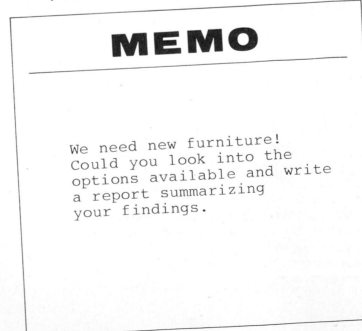

MEMO

We need new furniture! Could you look into the options available and write a report summarizing your findings.

Sample 7

For this week's tie-breaker, answer this question in no more than fifteen words:

In your opinion, could the present generation of office automation products be improved? If so, by what additions or changes?

Sample 8

Write a contribution in response to this question in the magazine *White Collar*:

White Collar, a new monthly aimed at young people in all types of office jobs, has a readers' opinion column which publishes contributions written in response to questions raised in the previous month's issue. In April one of the questions was:

Many professions and large organizations claim that, not only in terms of pay but also in terms of recruitment and advancement, men and women have opportunities which are genuinely equal. Many of our readers clearly think that this claim is not borne out in practice, and we agree that it is easy to point to instances of apparent hypocrisy where equality of opportunity is concerned. For example, the European Commission in Brussels openly criticises member governments for not introducing equal pay for equal work, while only 5·4% of the administrative grade posts in the Commission itself are occupied by women and there are no women at all in the top two ranks. Is there genuine equality where you work? Should there be such equality, or not? Give us your views and let us have your suggestions if you think the situation could be changed for the better.

Sample 9

Send in your favourite recipe to *Cook's Choice* by 15 August 1987. The best recipe will win a set of kitchen knives.

Task 2

Compare your numbering in Task 1 with another student's. What problems would you have in completing each of these writing tasks satisfactorily? Use this list to help you. Add any concerns of your own.

- knowledge of the world
- knowledge of the grammar
- knowledge of vocabulary
- being able to put simple sentences together
- understanding the task and knowing what is expected of you
- knowledge of how things are done in English (e.g., the form of a letter in English)
- getting ideas in order
- spelling and punctuation

Task 3

Now look at the samples again. Which, if any, of these tasks would you find difficult in your own language? Which would you find easy? Are your answers to these questions the same for English, or are they different?

Task 4

Work in small groups and decide whether you agree or disagree with the following statements:

- Writing well depends not only on knowing the grammar and the vocabulary of a language.
- It is easier to write about subjects which you are familiar with.
- Practice is an important element in writing well.
- Familiarity with examples of the same types of writing helps us to write our own.
- It helps to know why we are writing something.

2   Types of writing

The successful completion of a writing task usually requires the mastery of one or more types of writing.

Task 1

Which of the following types of writing is called for by each of the sample tasks? Complete the table below. (Some samples may require more than one type.)

type of writing	*sample*								
	1	2	3	4	5	6	7	8	9
narrative (or storytelling)									
personal correspondence	√								
business correspondence	√								
description									
explanation									
argument									
speeches									

These types of writing are all relevant to students at your level. Look at the table of contents to see which units develop the types of writing you want practice in. (The types of writing in samples 4 and 7 are covered in *Writing – Advanced* in this series.)

3 Looking at register and style

Task 1

Below are two letters. They are to the Managing Director of a company that sells diaries. One is polite and the other is quite rude. The two letters are mixed up. Can you separate them?

Dear Sir,

1 I am writing because, after several telephone calls, I still have not received the diary refill I ordered last November.
2 I wrote to your firm last November to order a refill for my diary.
3 When I telephoned I was assured that it had been sent but I am afraid that it still has not arrived.
4 Every time I telephone, an assistant tells me that it has been sent. Needless to say it has not arrived.
5 I appreciate that it may have been lost in the post.
6 I am tired of your excuses.
7 I would be grateful if you could send me another one as soon as possible.
8 Please make sure that a new diary is sent to me immediately.

Yours faithfully,

Discuss your answers in a small group.

When we are writing we have a purpose. It is very important that we choose a register that is appropriate to our purpose. For example, we should be sure that we are not impolite when we want to be polite. We also need to be careful about our style. For example, what is wrong with this letter to a bank manager?

Dear Sir,
Can you lend me some money this month because I have none.
Regards,
Mick

Apart from the missing information, such an informal letter is not appropriate in this context. It is important that you develop a sense of style. In each unit you will look at examples of an appropriate style for the type of writing being practised, but remember that you can improve your writing style by reading attentively.

4   Layout and organization

Read both versions of the following report quickly. You don't need to
understand all of it. Just decide which is the better version.

REPORT

The Housing Committee has had three meetings to discuss this matter and
a number of reports have been received from the Borough Surveyor and
the Legal Department.

Our Legal Department reports that there are no restrictions, i.e. no rights
of any kind and no encumbrances that would prevent building. But the site
does have some problems. It is a triangular block and this would mean
that those houses built close to the apex will have much smaller gardens
than those on the other side. We understand too that a few of the contractors in the town are not busy and we should expect some competitive
tenders.

Consequently we suggest that the Council should proceed to find out what
grants will be available, what the cost of building would be by taking some
provisional tenders.

The site does seem to be suitable for building and all the indications are
that it would take two- or three-storey houses. We have been informed by
the water, gas and electricity authorities that these services are all readily
available. We would recommend that the Council proceeds and decides
to build here because we have heard that private developers are interested
in the site.

PROPOSED HOUSING ON FOOTSWAY MEADOWS

INTRODUCTION

The Housing Committee has been asked to report to the Council on whether or not an estate should be
built on Footsway Meadows.

The Committee has had three meetings to discuss this matter and a number of reports have been received from the Borough Surveyor and the Legal Department.

LEGAL CONSIDERATIONS

Our Legal Department reports that there are no restrictions, i.e. no rights of any kind and no encumbrances that would prevent building.

THE SITE

There are some problems. The site is triangular and this would mean that those houses built close to
the apex will have much smaller gardens than those on the other side. But this is not a major drawback
and it does seem possible to build two- or three-storey houses. We have been informed by the water,
gas and electricity authorities that these services are all readily available.

THE CONTRACT

We understand that a few of the contractors in the town are not busy, so we should expect some competitive tenders.

CONCLUSION

We would recommend that the Council proceeds and decides to build here because we have heard that
private developers are interested in the site. We thus suggest the following next steps:

• the Council should find out what grants may be available.
• the Council should ask for tenders.

J. Knox
Chairman, Housing Committee

The second report is better and much easier to read. This is because it has better layout and organization:

- it has a title
- it has headings (including an introduction and a conclusion)
- it tries to group the material

All of this helps the reader who may not be interested in the whole report. Problems in layout and organization can easily be noticed when we look at reports and business letters but it is important to think about the way we order and group information in any form of writing.

5 Linking form and purpose

There are many different kinds of writing in English. Here is a list of some of them.

messages	talks
telegrams	textbooks
letters to the Editor	notes
letters to friends	reports
business letters	advertisements
postcards	articles
poems	instructions
diaries	memos
short stories	

Task 1

Work in pairs and decide whether the kinds of writing listed above are

- personal (and meant for the writer)
- public (and meant for other people)
- both.

When you have finished, compare and discuss your work with another pair. Did you finish with similar groupings? Report on your discussion to your teacher.

When we write we usually have a purpose in mind. It is our purpose and audience (i.e., the people who will read what we have written, even if it's ourselves) that influence our choice of expressions and words. This means different types of texts may well have different characteristic linguistic features.

Task 2

Look at these short extracts from longer texts and decide

- who you think they are written for
- what the texts are about
- why they were written.

2 Size of pan can help wise energy use. The panbase should just cover the cooker ring. If using gas, adjust the flame to suit the pan-size. Do not use a pan which is too big - or too small - for the contents.

1 Remove food or loose false teeth from the mouth. (Do not try to locate the object with your finger.) Encourage the victim to cough. It may be all that is needed to dislodge the blockage.

2 If this fails, help the victim to bend over with the head lower than the chest. He can be either sitting or standing. Slap him between the shoulder blades smartly with the heel of the hand up to four times. Each slap should be strong enough to dislodge the blockage.

3 Remember to put lids on saucepans, and turn down the heat once contents boil. Using the lid keeps heat in, reduces condensation and cuts down the energy waste.

4 Many things need just enough water in the pan to cover them. Too much water, or over-cooking, can both waste fuel and spoil food.

Now look at the above extracts again and discuss these questions in a small group:

1 What is the function of the two extracts?
2 Underline all the examples of the following:
   - The imperative form of verbs: e.g., *Remove food* . . .
   - Expressions to convey a condition: e.g., *If this fails, help the victim to* . . .
   - Phrases where the verb 'should' is used.
   How does the choice of verbs help to present the information clearly?
3 Why are the texts numbered?
4 What are the illustrations used for in each text?
5 Agree on five desirable characteristics for this kind of writing.

In this book we will examine the features of different kinds of writing so that you get a feel of what is appropriate for a particular purpose or audience.

6 Getting it right

Task 1

Look at this example of a piece of writing by a nine-year-old British girl. The girl was asked to write a narrative about a personal disaster to someone who has a travelling shop. Look at her first and second draft. (She has a lot of problems with spelling! To understand what she means read the text aloud to yourself.)

First draft

One day I went a little walk by my self wene I came back my engine was on fire I Phone the fire brigad they put water on it my van was all burnt I was very sade but I got a new van for nuthing I was very happy and I wasn't sade eny more.

Second draft

One day it was my tea brak it was a lovly day and I was very hot, I was by my self. I left the van in the cash incary* in the car park. wen I came out my engine was on fure. I phoned the fire brigad. thay came in ther van they got the fire hose out. my van was all burnt and I had to pay 200 punds for another van. I was very sade.

> **cash and carry** a large supermarket but only for people who own shops

Work in pairs and list the improvements she made in the second draft.

What are the problems that still remain? Discuss the suggestions you might make for her third draft. Write the third version and compare what you write with the work of another pair. Suggest improvements if you can.

Writing a narrative is a difficult task for adults! Did your suggested improvements include the following?

1 advice on how much detail to include (this will depend on how much the reader knows)
2 advice on how to make the story easy to follow by
   • using linkers and sequencers like *first, next, after that, afterwards, finally*, etc.
   • making the time relationships clear (e.g., by using the past perfect)
   • obeying the rules of spelling and punctuation

The girl is making progress towards being able to tell a story in writing, and we will look more at writing narrative in Unit 3. But remember that getting it right usually involves more than one draft. Unit 10 contains tasks to help you to edit your work, and although this is the last unit in the book, you might want to look at it during the entire course.

2

What goes in

1 Introduction

From time to time you may be asked to speak to a group of people in English. Most of us need careful preparation to do it well, and even the best speakers often start by writing out their talk in full. In this unit we will concentrate on the planning and writing of short talks in English.

2 Guidelines for preparing a talk

The important things to consider in preparing any talk are

the audience
- Who are they? What do you know about them? What do you need to know?
- What do they know about you? What do they need to know?
- What do they expect you to do or say?
- How much do they know about the subject already? How much do you need to tell them? How much can you tell them in the amount of time you have?

Answers to these questions will help you decide on the content of your introduction and talk.

the subject matter
What do you need to include (and exclude)?

The most important thing is to decide on a structure for the information you want to give. One 'rule' which is sometimes given is

Tell them what you are going to say — say it — tell them what you've said.

This means that many talks have
- an *introduction* where, if necessary, you tell the audience
  who you are
  why you are talking to them
  what you will be talking about
  what they have to do (for example, do they need to listen carefully and write information down, will you give them a summary, etc.)
- a *middle* where it is important to be logical so that you present your information clearly and in stages
- an *end* which may be a summary of the main points and a reminder or check of what they must do.

(The oral presentation of talks is dealt with in *Speaking – Elementary* and *Upper-intermediate* in this series.)

Remember that although it's important to write down what you want to say you shouldn't read from a prepared text, so always rehearse your speech or talk if you can. In this way you will sound natural.

3 Structuring information

The first step in preparing a talk is to structure the information.
Look back at page 6 before you continue.

Task 1

Read the two examples of announcements below. Which example
would be easier to follow and more likely to work? Why? List your
reasons.

Announcement A
'OK! Erm, the buses leave at 3.00 right. So make sure you get to the
meeting point by 2.45 er, no let's make it 2.30 as there are a lot of you to
get on board and we had that trouble last time. Now if you're not there
we're not going to wait! It's very inconsiderate to keep everyone waiting.
Oh yes, the meeting point is not the same as the usual one outside the
school. We're meeting outside the sports hall. OK. Now I'd like to, to talk
to you about . . .'

Announcement B
'Right. Can I have your attention please. (pause) We're going to meet for
our excursion at 2.30 p.m. I'll repeat that, 2.30 p.m. Today the buses will
leave from the sports hall. That's right, the sports hall. Not the school.
Now we can't wait for people who are late so make sure you get there on
time. Any questions?'

Task 2

Many announcements seek to give us instructions. List six criteria
for good instructions: for example, *Good instructions should be easy to
understand*. Then compare your criteria with the list on the next
page.

1   Adequate explanation. You should be told what you have to do.
2   Clarity. The instructions should be clear so they are easy to understand.
3   Economy. The aim is to be as simple as possible and not say more than you have to.
4   Completeness. Nothing must be left out.
5   Accuracy. You don't want the person giving instructions to make a mistake.
6   Logical ordering. You want things in the best order, e.g., the order in which things are to be done.

The need for qualities like clarity are most obvious when we're preparing instructions, but unless we're producing imaginative writing we should always have these criteria in mind whenever we write. The aim should always be to produce clear, accurate work that is effectively ordered for our purpose. The best way to make an announcement that is well structured is to start by writing down what you want to say.

Task 3

Imagine that you have to welcome a group of visitors to a hotel. During the day you've made notes in the list below of the things you have to tell them. Group your ideas under four or five headings.

Breakfast is served in the dining room from 7.30 to 9.30 a.m.
Welcome drink in the lounge at 7.30 p.m.
Keys are available from reception.
Dinner starts at 8.00 and is normally served up till 10.30 p.m.
Registration forms have been completed. Just sign them when you get your key.
Rooms are on third and fourth floor.
Baggage will be brought to your room.
The hotel offers snooker, tennis, table tennis, a swimming pool and a sauna.
First excursion at 10.00 a.m. tomorrow.
Full programme on the notice-board everyday.
Lunch is not provided at the hotel.
Lounge and residents' bar on the first floor.
Available to answer questions in lobby before dinner every evening.
Book for sauna etc. at the hall porter.

Task 4

Now use the notes and headings from Task 3 to write out a short welcoming talk. Look through the following checklist while you're preparing it.

1   This is the first time you have met this group, who have just arrived in your town. Make sure you welcome them and make the necessary introductions. The following expressions might be useful:

'Ladies and gentlemen, I'd like to welcome you to . . .'
'I'll start by introducing myself. My name is . . .'
'I'd like to make a few brief announcements . . .'

2   Choose the best order to present your information. What do the visitors have to do first? What information is best left to the end?
3   Make sure that you use expressions like *and, right, so,* and *as you know* to link your sentences.

Compare your work with two or three other students.
Did you choose the same order? Does it matter in this case?
Did you manage to present the information without using too many words?

4   Selection and organization

When we write we sometimes start with too many ideas. Even when ideas are difficult to find it's worth putting them down so that we can select and organize the content of what we write. Any communication which is too long and full of irrelevant information will be inefficient.

Task 1

Look at this list of suggestions provided by a group of students when they were asked for ideas on how to convince students that discussion lessons are not a waste of time. Decide on the suggestions that you think are useful and remove any that you think are of little use.

Some ideas for making discussion lessons successful
Make sure people want to come; give them food and drink
Keep everyone interested
Tell everyone the subject of the discussion before they start
Elect a chairperson each time the class meets
Ask students if there is anything they would like to discuss
Give everyone a chance to speak
Make the lesson enjoyable
Only discuss things which are important
Agree on a specific length of time for discussion
Record discussions on tape or video
Stop people who talk too much from taking part
Invite people from outside the class
Have lessons in a comfortable place
Make sure everyone can see the other members of the class
Use audio-visual equipment
Have a strong chairperson
Prepare an agenda
Listen to what other people say
Have discussion lessons in the garden in summer

When you have finished add any ideas of your own.

Task 2

Assume that you have to give a talk on 'How to make the most of discussion lessons' to students at a lower level.

Arrange the ideas you've kept in an effective order. To do this you should group similar suggestions together and decide on an order of presentation.

Compare your work in a small group. Make a note of any similarities or differences and be ready to present the results of your discussion to the whole class.

5   Choosing your words carefully

In any form of communication we need to choose our words carefully.

Task 1

Read these two extracts from the beginning of a talk and discuss the questions that follow them.

Extract A
Sorry to be late! I couldn't park. Well, here we are! As I'm at the Institute of Directors my subject tonight is 'industrial relations', right! I mean they're really awful in this country. Aren't they? Management sits in their office; the workers go on strike at the slightest excuse. It's diabolical. Now if you take Japan, things are different there . . .

Extract B
A century and a half ago, Charles Lamb, the famous English writer, was walking along a London street with a friend. And he stopped and pointed. 'Do you see that man over there?' he said, 'I hate him.' 'Hate him?' his friend said, 'How can you hate him? You don't even know who he is.' And Lamb said: 'Precisely.'

We have all seen tragic examples of this very kind of hate born of ignorance — both within our country and without and beyond. In certain languages the word for 'enemy' is 'stranger'. The problem comes down to 'precisely' that alluded to by Charles Lamb. We don't know our fellow men!

And I suggest that you and I must make it our business to correct this. I believe our one great hope is the dissemination of knowledge. That is why, when the International Institute of Education and through them, you good people, asked me to come to . . .

1   What is the subject of each of the talks?
2   How does the speaker in Extract **A** begin the talk?
3   How does the speaker in Extract **B** begin?
4   Which is more appropriate/effective, **A** or **B**? Why?
5   How could the speaker in **A** sound more polite?

Choosing the right words for what we want to say is an important part of appropriacy. And we always need to think about our audience. In the next task you will get some practice in this.

Task 2

A popular English colleague who has been in your organization for more than ten years has decided to return to Britain in order to get married. It happens that the person will not be replaced. You have been asked to give a speech at your colleague's farewell party.

Look at this first draft of the talk. The words and expressions in italics could be made more appropriate or omitted altogether. Work in pairs to improve the talk. You may want to change the order of some of the sentences.

Ladies and gentlemen. As you all know we are gathered here tonight to say farewell to *one of our foreign employees*. Susan has been with the research division of this company for *at least ten years, maybe more* . . . As some of you may know, Susan is going back to England in order to get married *at last*. We will all miss her very much *but are delighted that she is leaving us now as she will not be replaced*. Susan's research project which has been completed has been a great success. *I would like to offer you good wishes* for the future.

Task 3

You have joined a new multinational company. One of its traditions is that new employees are asked to introduce themselves briefly during the regular meetings. You should aim to say a few words about your background, qualifications and experience and special interests.

Make notes of all the information that you want to include.
Write a first draft of your talk.

Look through your talk and make sure the information is logically ordered.

Look through the talk again. Do the majority of your sentences start with 'I'? This can make you sound very self-centred. See if you can use some alternatives like:

My career started . . .	*Before long* . . .
After leaving University . . .	*My previous job was* . . .
My next job was with . . .	*My husband and I enjoy sailing* . . .
After staying in the job for . . .	

Write a second draft of your talk.
Now form a small group and exchange talks. Decide whether each talk is
- clear
- well-ordered
- easy to listen to.

Task 4

Choose one of the following topics **A** or **B**. You are going to write a short talk of approximately 100 words. In writing your talk you should
- decide on the audience; who are they and what is their background?
- make notes on all the information that you want to include
- order the information so that it's clear and logical
- try and check that the words and expressions you want to use are appropriate
- think carefully about how to start and end the talk.

Topic A
You have been asked to say a few words of introduction to a group of foreign visitors to your home town (or a town that you know well). It will help them to know a few simple facts about the town, its history, the places you can visit, etc. Mention things which are unique or of special interest. You don't need to talk about hotels, meals, etc., as another speaker will mention these.

Topic B
You have been asked to speak to a group of British businessmen. They are interested in information about your organization or school but they know very little about your country. Write the talk you would give.

Task 5

Work in small groups and exchange scripts with each other. Read the talks you wrote in Task 4.

In your first reading find all the grammar and spelling mistakes. Decide whether the choice of words can be improved.

Read the talks again and decide whether the organization can be improved.

Decide whether the expressions used are appropriate for the people you're talking to.

Make a note of any areas that you're unsure of, such as spellings or the use of a particular tense, and consult your teacher or a reference book.

Make a list of areas for improvement.

1 Introduction

> **narrative** n. **1** tale, story, recital of facts; kind of composition or talk that confines itself to these

3

Putting it together

Task 1

Look at these examples of composition exercises, which are typical of those in the *Cambridge First Certificate Examination*. Which ones require a narrative?

1 Describe the achievement and influence of any important compatriot of yours.
2 What are the advantages and disadvantages of air travel?
3 You hear that a friend of yours has been sent to prison for theft. A month later he tells you it was all a mistake. Write his story.
4 It is sometimes said many of our problems would disappear if the world spoke one language. Do you agree?
5 Give an account of your visit to a world-famous sport or entertainment event.

Discuss your ideas for each composition in a small group.

Task 2

When you reach this level of English you are expected to be able to write a good narrative. A good written narrative is basically a good story. Work in pairs and make a list of the characteristics you think should go into a good story. Share your ideas with other students before reading the discussion below.

The ingredients of a good story may include originality, humour, suspense and a vivid description, but the first essential for a good narrative is the ability to link and sequence a series of events so that it is easy for your reader to follow you. This unit concentrates on how you can use grammar to achieve this.

2 Assess your approach

Task 1

Assess your approach to narrative with the help of this questionnaire.

When you write a narrative . . .

1   do you decide who you are writing for?
    always ☐ *sometimes* ☐ *never* ☐
2   do you list all your ideas before you start?
    always ☐ *sometimes* ☐ *never* ☐
3   do you organize your ideas so that your story has a structure
    (e.g., a beginning, a middle and an end) before you start?
    always ☐ *sometimes* ☐ *never* ☐
4   do you write a first draft?
    always ☐ *sometimes* ☐ *never* ☐
5   do you correct and improve on what you have written?
    always ☐ *sometimes* ☐ *never* ☐

The way we write is very personal, but most people would agree that
it's worth following each of these stages when we are learning to
write in a foreign language. It is particularly important that we know
who we are writing for or to. Outside the classroom this is not a
problem: we don't usually write unless we have a reason. In the
classroom this may be different.

The instructions for some exercises may tell us who the reader is.
In other cases we have to imagine one. If you are asked to write
narrative, but you are not told who you are writing for, you must
invent an audience. One way to overcome this problem may be to put
your narrative in a letter to a 'friend'.

3 Telling a story

The tasks in this section give practice in the grammatical devices
which are essential to story-telling. Do as many of these tasks as
possible. Some of them could be done at home.

Task 1

Look at this example of a letter from a woman's magazine. It tells the
story of something that happened to a reader. Notice how the
expressions in italics make the sequence of events clear.

Memory Man
I give the occasional evening demonstration in village halls all over
Suffolk and Essex. *One nasty night, after* a long drive, I reached a village
crossroads and was totally confused. Should I turn left or right for the
village hall? *While* I was sitting wondering a bent old man emerged from a
tiny pub on the corner and stared at me as I wound the window down to

ask him the way. *Before* I could say a word, he shouted across, 'I told you last time you came here, two or three years ago, where the hall was. You don't listen, do you!'

Now imagine you are the old man. Write the story he might tell his friends in the pub. Exchange stories with two other students. Did you use similar expressions to sequence your story or not? How did the story change according to the audience?

Task 2

Nasreddin Hodja is one of the most celebrated personalities of the Middle East, the Balkans and Greece, and there are a lot of stories about him. In many of these stories the Hodja is made to say or do things which are remarkably intelligent, and on other occasions he does things which are very stupid. The main purpose of the stories is to make people laugh and think.

Read the following version of a story about the Hodja, and discuss the function of the words and expressions in italics. Can you suggest alternatives for any of them?

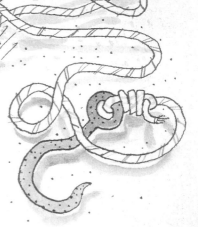

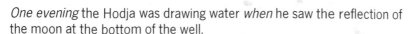

One evening the Hodja was drawing water *when* he saw the reflection of the moon at the bottom of the well.

'The moon has fallen down my well,' said the Hodja. 'If I do not get it out, it will be the end of the world, and everyone will blame me!'

So he tied a large iron hook to the end of a piece of rope, and let it down the well. *When* he judged that he could hook the moon, he began to pull on the rope. The hook, *however had caught* under a stone at the bottom of the well. The Hodja strained and pulled, *until* the hook suddenly dislodged the stone and flew up the well-shaft. The Hodja fell flat on his own back. 'Allah be praised!' he said, seeing the moon in the sky. 'It was a great effort, but I have got it back where it belongs.'

Use the notes below to write your own version of a Nasreddin Hodja story. Make sure you use appropriate sequencers and linkers.

a poor man passing through Ak Sehir — only had piece of dry bread to eat — saw some meatballs in a pan on fire — smell was delicious — held bread over fire — restaurant owner had seen this — took man to see the Hodja who was the judge — asked for price of meatballs — Hodja listened — took coins from pocket — rattled them in restaurant owner's ear — owner surprised and angry — Hodja explained — 'The sound of money is fair payment for the smell of food'

Join a small group of students and read what you have written to each other. Do you prefer any of the versions to the others? Why? Compare your version to the original which is on page 85.

Task 3

Read this extract carefully and try to reconstruct the missing parts of the text.

Locking grandma in a cupboard

My earliest memory was (1) . . . .
When I (2) . . . . a little girl and my mother was expecting my brother, my grandma (3) . . . . to our house for the day. Under the stairs we had a cupboard in which we kept our brushes and mops. My grandma (4) . . . . into the cupboard for something, and as I had a habit of closing doors I saw the door open and (5) . . . . I then ran out to play. When my grandma found out she was locked in (6) . . . . Hearing her upstairs my mother said she would get up and let her out. My grandma not allowing my mother to get up said (7) . . . . till my dad came home.

  My mum (8) . . . . what she could do when she heard the old man next door; she shouted out of the window for him. She told him to (9) . . . . , so he let her out. When I (10) . . . . I got a clout but everybody thought it was funny.

Discuss your work in pairs or small groups before looking at the key.

Now answer these questions:

1 What is the difference between the simple past, the past perfect and the past continuous?
2 What are the rules for reported speech?

Make sure that you know how these operate as they are very important in good narrative.

Task 4

In pairs, look at the pictures below. Use them to help you to write a
100 to 150 word story. You can use the pictures in any sequence, and
you can add any detail you want.

Join another pair and compare the stories you have written. Then do
the following:

- Make a list of all the expressions used to sequence the events in
  your story.
- Decide if you can use alternatives for any of the expressions.
- Make a list of *all* the expressions used or discussed with the help
  of your teacher.

4   Describing traditional customs

Task 1

Look at this photograph of an unusual British custom which dates back hundreds of years. Can you guess what the event is? Does it remind you of a past or present event in your own country? Try to imagine what the event might be and write a short description in pairs before reading the actual description.

Weighing the Mayor

A strange ceremony marks the beginning of the civic year in High Wycombe. The town has had mayors since 1285 and the custom of Weighing the Mayor has survived. At 6.30 on a Thursday evening towards the end of May a procession of dignitaries goes along the High Street to the Town Hall where the new mayor takes office. Immediately afterwards they assemble outside where a comfortable looking chair is attached to a fine old scale which is suspended from a brass tripod.

The mayor is weighed first, followed by the mayoress, the ex-mayor and so on. The weights are checked and recorded, and announced by an official. Each announcement of the weight is followed by the words 'and no more' or 'and some more', depending on whether the official has lost or gained weight in the past year. A loss of weight signifies hard work over the past year, a gain, laziness. Consequently he or she is cheered or booed as appropriate.

When does the ceremony take place?
Where does it happen?
What is the procedure for the ceremony? Underline the words and phrases which help you to follow the procedure.

Task 2

Describing a custom or event is a form of narrative. We need to describe where and when it takes place, what happens, and so on. Write a description of a custom in your own country. This can be real or imaginary but you must convince the other students that it is real. Look at the language in the passage *Weighing the Mayor*. Make sure that you

- describe the event in sequence by using time words and phrases like *At 12 o'clock*, and *In the evening*.
- use the present tense where appropriate.

Read your description to the other members of a small group. See if they can guess whether the custom is real or imaginary. Choose the most interesting description and work together to improve it before getting a member of your group to read it to the class.

5   A memorable experience

Task 1

Look at these illustrations.

Do they remind you of something you won't forget? If not, is there a holiday, a sports event, or an incident that you find particularly memorable?

Choose one memorable experience and prepare to write a 150 word narrative about it. Imagine that the narrative is part of a personal letter to a good friend.
Follow the procedure below.

1   Make notes about the event you have chosen.
2   Organize your notes into sections
    Decide on a few useful linkers and phrases you would like to include.
3   Write the first draft.
4   Underline any sections that you want to change and discuss these with a partner.
5   Write your composition.
6   Read through the final version. Concentrate on your
    - grammar (especially tenses and linkers)
    - choice of words
    - spelling
    - organization
    - punctuation

Making things clear

1 Introduction

When we are presenting information it is very important that we do it as clearly and simply as possible. This is true for all forms of written and oral communication. In this unit we will concentrate on instructions and the sort of information presented in brochures and leaflets. Remember, however, that the same principles apply to other forms of writing. As the critic and author Matthew Arnold said:

'People think I can teach them style. What stuff it is. Have something to say and say it as clearly as you can. That is the only secret of style.'

2 Is it clear?

Task 1

Look at the following extracts form different brochures and leaflets and complete the grid below them. Put a tick (√) in the box if you think the extract meets the criteria on the left. Put a cross (×) if you think it doesn't. Discuss your answers in a small group.

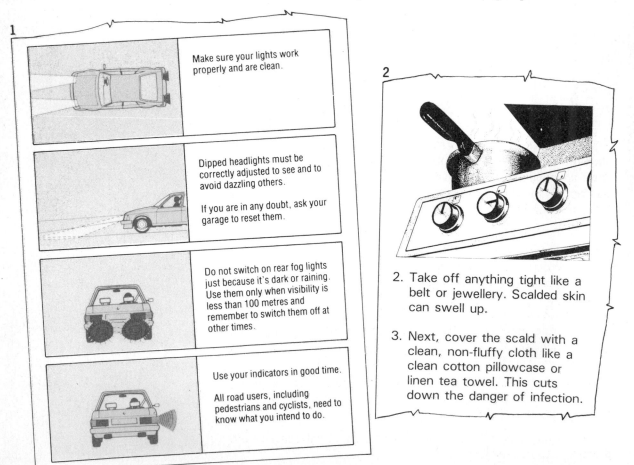

1

Make sure your lights work properly and are clean.

Dipped headlights must be correctly adjusted to see and to avoid dazzling others.

If you are in any doubt, ask your garage to reset them.

Do not switch on rear fog lights just because it's dark or raining. Use them only when visibility is less than 100 metres and remember to switch them off at other times.

Use your indicators in good time.

All road users, including pedestrians and cyclists, need to know what you intend to do.

2

2. Take off anything tight like a belt or jewellery. Scalded skin can swell up.

3. Next, cover the scald with a clean, non-fluffy cloth like a clean cotton pillowcase or linen tea towel. This cuts down the danger of infection.

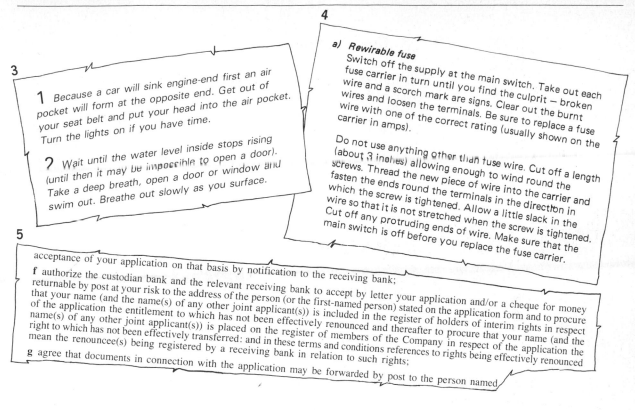

4

a) Rewirable fuse
Switch off the supply at the main switch. Take out each fuse carrier in turn until you find the culprit – broken wire and a scorch mark are signs. Clear out the burnt wires and loosen the terminals. Be sure to replace a fuse wire with one of the correct rating (usually shown on the carrier in amps).

Do not use anything other than fuse wire. Cut off a length (about 3 inches) allowing enough to wind round the screws. Thread the new piece of wire into the carrier and fasten the ends round the terminals in the direction in which the screw is tightened. Allow a little slack in the wire so that it is not stretched when the screw is tightened. Cut off any protruding ends of wire. Make sure that the main switch is off before you replace the fuse carrier.

3

1 Because a car will sink engine-end first an air pocket will form at the opposite end. Get out of your seat belt and put your head into the air pocket. Turn the lights on if you have time.

2 Wait until the water level inside stops rising (until then it may be impossible to open a door). Take a deep breath, open a door or window and swim out. Breathe out slowly as you surface.

5

acceptance of your application on that basis by notification to the receiving bank;
f authorize the custodian bank and the relevant receiving bank to accept by letter your application and/or a cheque for money returnable by post at your risk to the address of the person (or the first-named person) stated on the application form and to procure that your name (and the name(s) of any other joint applicant(s)) is included in the register of holders of interim rights in respect of the application the entitlement to which has not been effectively renounced and thereafter to procure that your name (and the name(s) of any other joint applicant(s)) is placed on the register of members of the Company in respect of the application the right to which has not been effectively transferred: and in these terms and conditions references to rights being effectively renounced mean the renouncee(s) being registered by a receiving bank in relation to such rights;
g agree that documents in connection with the application may be forwarded by post to the person named

criteria	*extract*				
	1	2	3	4	5
The text is easy to read					
The important information is easy to find					
The material looks interesting					
Any illustrations are clear and helpful					
The layout (the way the illustrations and text appear on the page) is clear					

Now look at the extracts again. Which ones observe the following 'rules' for clear writing?

1 Use common words such as 'end' rather than 'terminate' or 'try' rather than 'endeavour', where possible.
2 Use short sentences (the average is usually between ten and twenty words).
3 Introduce only one new piece of information in a sentence.
4 Do not artificially shorten sentences by leaving out words like 'a' 'the' and 'that'.
5 Follow the usual English word order of subject, verb and object (if there is one).
6 Organize the information logically.

Following these 'rules' will make any written information you want to present easier to read!

3   Headings can help

Headings and titles can help your reader get straight to the main point of the section which follows.

Task 1

Look at these extracts from a booklet advertising the new *Sony Video 8* system. Three of the section titles have been removed. Work in pairs and replace them.

TAKE A CLOSER LOOK AT THE WORLD'S MOST POPULAR CAMCORDER

You are now looking at the world's most popular camcorder – Sony's CCD V8AF. It's the same camcorder that 'What Video?' magazine chose as the 'BEST CAMCORDER OF 1985'. What makes the CCD V8AF so highly rated?

Features such as infra-red Auto Focus allow the keen videographer to concentrate on the creative opportunities of the shot, knowing that it will be pin-sharp and perfectly focussed. A six times powered motor zoom lens ensures sharp close-ups, too. And don't worry about pointing into the sun; the CCD V8AF – like the Handycam – incorporates a CCD Imager chip, not a tube, to eliminate the problem of glare and comet tails.

What's more, the viewfinder can be adjusted for the left or right eye and even has a facility to allow you to take a close look at a scene at a flip of the eyepiece.

SHOOT AND REVIEW

After you've shot the scene you don't have to move on and just hope for the best – you can review it immediately on the electronic viewfinder with an instant playback, at either normal or fast-forward speed. A record review feature allows you to double check your last segment of recording before starting the next shot. So you can't go wrong. The CCD V8AF even allows you to 'freeze frame' so you can study a particular piece of footage.

Once you're satisfied that you have finished shooting your epic, you can play back your pictures on any TV – you just plug the camcorder directly into the aerial socket of the set. The CCD V8AF also gives you an editing switch for simple editing onto another VCR, and the unidirectional microphone ensures that you pick up the best possible sound. An SP/LP mode switch gives up to 3 hours of recording time from a P5 90 cassette.

At just 2.3 kilograms, the CCD V8AF is as light and portable as it is stylish. You can shoot comfortably from the shoulder for that professional 'camera angle' and find all the essential controls at your fingertips.

The CCD V8AF comes complete with a strong yet lightweight carrying case which can fit easily under an airline seat. Other supplied accessories include a Battery, AC Power Adaptor, Battery Charger and a 30 minute tape. A full range of other add-on extras you can see on pages 18 and 19.

Now you know why it's the world's most popular camcorder. Go and see it for yourself.

You can check your answers on page 85.

Task 2

Sometimes writers fail to section their material at all.
Read the extract below from a brochure about Lake Balaton in
Hungary. Separate the material into sections which deal with the
same topic and rewrite the extract giving each section a title, such as
Electricity, Visas, etc. You may change the order within the extract
if you wish. Try and simplify any sections which are difficult to read.

DESTINATION: LAKE BALATON – A TRIP TO A JOLLY RECREATION LAND

To swimmers, sunbathers, and aquatic sports enthusiasts, Lake Balaton is a generous gift of nature. White and multicoloured sails glide over the sun-reflecting water, and the waves splash in the wake of the water skiers. Laughter and the noise of carefree play sound from the beaches, from the endless chain of colourful camping sites, and from the parks with their shadow-casting trees.

Out of the water rise blue mountains with sloping vineyards where in old press houses the grapes are squashed that make the sparkling wine stored in the cellars of this famous region.

Hidden in the valleys reaching out to the lake, there are the famous castle ruins, the small towns with their tiny baroque mansions, their statues carved in stone and their moss-covered mills. There they are—the gently rolling hills, the old csárdas (village pubs), the lovely hamlets with their white-washed houses. There is charm, there is romance in the air.

Relaxation, rest and well-balanced exercise, harmony of past and present, interesting excursions and entertainment—this is Lake Balaton for you.

Lake Balaton, situated in Transdanubia, the Western part of Hungary, is the largest lake of Central and Western Europe. It covers an area of about 600 square kilometers, measuring 77 km in length and between two and 14 km in width.

The shoreline is 197 km and the lake's average depth is 3 m; the shallow water and the sandy shore in the South are ideal for families with small children. In summer, the water quickly warms up to a temperature of 21–27°C. In spring, the first sun rays attract swimmers to the beach and the season lasts far into September.

But the most beautiful time is autumn. Those who do not mind bathing in water below 22°C might enjoy the pleasures of summer merged with the gorgeous colours and moods of autumn.

The temperature of the lake is rather steady, the air—because of the surrounding forest-covered mountains—is clear as well as dust-free, and only moderately humid. The sun shines particularly bright because it is reflected on the water and contains plenty of ultra-violet rays.

The lake abounds in fish. The local speciality is fogas (perch-pike) which is called süllö when young. Other sophisticated fish such as glanis or carp are also available.

A sudden storm at Lake Balaton is indeed an event of great fascination to watch. Rockets in vivid colours warn swimmers and people out sailing in good time of the approaching danger.

Lake Balaton is 90 kilometres west of Budapest. From there it may be reached by car on the M-7 motorway.

The distance between Lake Balaton and

Amsterdam:	1,524 kilometres
Berlin:	994 kilometres
Calais:	1,674 kilometres
Cologne:	1,243 kilometres
Hamburg:	1,224 kilometres
Innsbruck:	823 kilometres
Kiel:	1,320 kilometres
Moscow:	2,020 kilometres
Munich:	786 kilometres
Paris:	1,613 kilometres
Rotterdam:	1,497 kilometres
Rome:	1,407 kilometres
Venice:	856 kilometres
Zurich:	1,112 kilometres

Guests going to Budapest by express train, hydrofoil or plane may continue their swift and comfortable journey to Lake Balaton by taking one of the many express trains, motorcoaches, or hired cars (rent-a-car service, with or without driver, from travel agencies).

Tourists wishing to travel by train may obtain from their local travel agent a discount tourist season ticket valid for 10, 20 or 30 days on all lines of the Hungarian State Railways.

A valid passport and visa are required for entering Hungary. The visa may be obtained at any of the Hungarian diplomatic representations. Tourists arriving by car or by air may obtain a tourist visa without too much delay at the border or at the airport. Tourist visas are issued on condition that the recipient exchanges convertible currency equivalent to a minimum of 150 Forints a day for the whole period of their stay, or that the possession of vouchers issued by a trave... y abroad as proof that the require... m has been paid for.

People dress about the same way as in other European countries. On official occasions, in restaurants or places of entertainment, men wear lounge suits, and ladies cocktail dresses—except on very hot summer days. In spring and autumn, it is advisible to add warm clothing to the light summer wardrobe because the temperature may change rapidly.

In Hungary, including Lake Balaton, there is A.C. 220 V 50 A both in hotels and other places of accommodation.

For letters up to 20 grams to Western European and to overseas countries a 3 Forint stamp is needed; postcards require a 2 Forint stamp. The speed limit for cars in built-up areas is 60 km/h. Outside built-up areas it is 100 km/h, on motorways it is 120 km/h.

When you have finished discuss these questions in small groups:

1 Did you all have the same number of sections? Make a note of any disagreements.
2 Did you choose to simplify the same sections of the text? Read the sections you have simplified to each other. Choose the best versions.

Choose one member of your group to report your discussion to the rest of the class.

4   Giving advice

Task 1

Look at the texts on pages 24 and 25. Identify the texts which aim to give advice and complete the following task.

1   A lot of the verb forms are in the imperative. Write down two examples.
2   Find and list examples of verbs which mean the same as *make sure*.
3   We often emphasize what we want to say by using adverbs such as *always*. See if you can find any examples.

(See also page 8 in Unit 1)

Task 2

In this task you will work in a small group in order to produce some written advice for a group of English adults who are about to learn a foreign language for the first time. They will study in the same kind of school you are in and your objective is to help them. You have a maximum of two pages.
Follow this procedure:

1   Start by working individually. Write down all the information you would want to include.
2   Share your ideas with your colleagues.
3   Make a list of the headings you will use. Put the headings in a logical order.
4   Work together to produce a text which is as clear and logical as possible.
5   Exchange your work with another group. Does the text meet most of the criteria established in Section 2?
    Be ready to tell the other group
    • how their text might be improved
    • what you like about it.

5   Get your instructions right

Good instructions follow many of the 'rules' we have already looked
at, such as clarity and economy. But they also have to be complete!

Task 1

Look at this recipe for fresh tomato sauce with pasta. Some of the
steps are missing and this might cause problems for an inexperienced
cook. Read the recipe and see if you can discover what is missing.

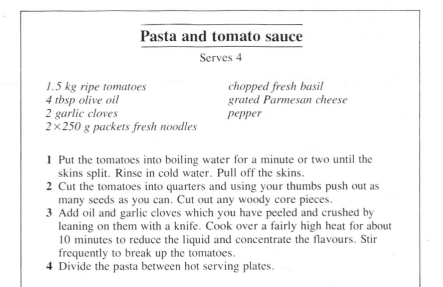

Pasta and tomato sauce
Serves 4

1.5 kg ripe tomatoes   *chopped fresh basil*
4 tbsp olive oil   *grated Parmesan cheese*
2 garlic cloves   *pepper*
2×250 g packets fresh noodles

1 Put the tomatoes into boiling water for a minute or two until the
  skins split. Rinse in cold water. Pull off the skins.
2 Cut the tomatoes into quarters and using your thumbs push out as
  many seeds as you can. Cut out any woody core pieces.
3 Add oil and garlic cloves which you have peeled and crushed by
  leaning on them with a knife. Cook over a fairly high heat for about
  10 minutes to reduce the liquid and concentrate the flavours. Stir
  frequently to break up the tomatoes.
4 Divide the pasta between hot serving plates.

Discuss your answer with a partner before reading the commentary
below.

Commentary

Two sentences were omitted from the recipe. The instruction 'Put
the tomatoes into a frying pan' should be added to the end of stage 2
and there should be an instruction to cook the pasta in stage 4. Did
you find these 'mistakes', or any others? If you didn't find the second
mistake this may be because you didn't know that you have to cook
pasta, or you are so familiar with it that you didn't feel it was worth
mentioning. The result might be cold pasta! Note also the following
points:
• Recipes are usually written in the imperative form to make sure
  they are clear.
• Sentences are short and contain one or two main ideas.
• It is very important that you use the appropriate verbs to describe
  the process of cooking. If you look at the example here you will
  find verbs like 'rinse' and 'reduce' that have precise meanings in
  cookery. Using the right word makes the instructions more
  economical.

Task 2

One way to find the right word is to use a thesaurus. A thesaurus is a reference book which groups words with similar or related meanings together.

If you look up the word 'cook' in the index of *Roget's Thesaurus*, you find

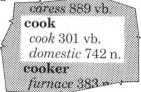

caress 889 vb.
cook
   cook 301 vb.
   domestic 742 n.
cooker
furnace 383 n.

vb. indicates the use of the word 'cook' as a verb.
n. indicates its use as a noun.
The number gives the section you want.

Section 301 is the section for food. In it there is a subsection of verbs related to food and the entry for the verb 'to cook' is as follows:

banquet, have to dinner 882 vb.
hospitable.

   cook, do to a turn; bake, scallop; roast, spit; broil, grill, griddle, devil, curry; sauté, fry; scramble, poach; boil, parboil; coddle, seethe; simmer, steam; casserole, stew; baste, lard; mince, dice; stuff, dress, garnish; sauce, flavour, spice.

302. Ex

You would have found the same entry if you had looked up a related word like 'grill'.

The problem with a thesaurus is choosing what you need. Some of these entries, like 'coddle', 'griddle' and 'scallop', are very unusual and you wouldn't need to have them as part of your vocabulary unless you are extremely interested in food. Other terms like 'roast', 'scramble' and 'steam' are common and used frequently. Discuss the meaning of the entries for 'to cook' that you are interested in before going on to Task 3. Use a dictionary if you have one.

Task 3

Work with a partner. Aim to write complete instructions for a recipe for a national dish.
Before you start make sure you have the vocabulary you need.
Follow the format of the recipe in Task 1. Show your final recipe to the other students.
Is the recipe clear and easy to follow?
Have you included all the important stages?

6 Presenting your own information

Task 1

The aim of this task is for you to present tourist information about
the town you are living in. If you are living in Britain the information
could be for foreign students of your age. If you are living outside
Britain the information might be for English speaking tourists. Try to
find a group of people who would be interested in reading what you
will write.

Your teacher will divide you into small groups and give you a large
piece of paper. You should aim to present all your information on one
sheet.

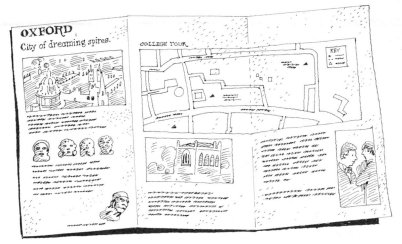

Procedure
Hold a group meeting to decide on the content of your sheet. During
the meeting you must decide
• what information to include: local customs, best restaurants, etc.
• how to illustrate your broadsheet: maps, photographs, etc.
• who will do what: who will research the different sections, find the
  photographs, etc.

After a period of time your teacher will give you a chance to meet
again to look at the information you have written and gathered. This
time you should meet as a group to
• check that the information (and the English!) is accurate
• decide exactly what you will include
• produce your broadsheet.

MAKE SURE THAT THE INFORMATION IS CLEARLY AND
EFFECTIVELY PRESENTED.

When you have finished you should display your work for the other
members of the class.
Walk round and discuss each sheet.

5

Getting things done

1 Introduction

One of the main functions of personal business letters is to get something done. These are some of the reasons for writing business letters:

- to complain about a product or service
- to get action on a problem: for example, you want the tourist board to offer better facilities for foreign visitors
- to ask for information
- to make a routine request
- to confirm a conversation

Our ability to write as well as read and understand business correspondence is helped by the existence of conventions. There are standard ways to
- lay out a business letter
- begin and end letters
- structure the information: for example, by starting with the most important point.

These conventions are not 'rules'; they can be broken. The main thing is to get your message across and following conventions does help your reader to find important information more easily. The aim of this unit is to introduce you to the strategies of effective personal business letters.

Task 1

Look at this example of a standard personal business letter and complete the statements on the next page.

```
                                              27 Woodland Court
                                              Woodbridge
                                              Surrey   SY1 5EJ        ———1

Peter Brown                                   11 June 1987
Greneral Manager
Sun Insurance Company
PO Box 200                                    Your ref: HP 135650      ———3
Sun House
London SW1 1GH

Dear Mr Brown

                    Additional premiums                                ———5

    I have pleasure in enclosing a cheque for £50 which represents
6—  the additional premium requested in your letter of
    1 June 1987.

    I would be grateful if you could acknowledge receipt of
    this letter.

    Yours sincerely

    R. Bassenthwaite

4—  Roger Bassenthwaite
```

1   Always putting your address in the top right-hand corner makes it easy for the reader to . . . . . .

2   Having the name and address of the person you are writing to on the letter means that even if the envelope is opened in another office . . . . . .

3   Putting the reference number down will help . . . . in their files.

4   Printing your name under your signature . . . . . .

5   The heading immediately under 'Dear _____' tells the reader . . . . . .

6   The function of the first sentence is to . . . . . .

Discuss your statements with a partner or with the class before looking at the key on page 85.

Task 2

This should be a revision task. Try and complete it as quickly as possible.
Use the examples of letters on pages 38 and 41 to help you if necessary.

1   What are the rules for English addresses?
    Which of the following comes first?

    ☐   the town
    ☐   the street name
    ☐   the number

2   Write today's date in three ways which are acceptable in English.

3   Letters usually start with a salutation or greeting, such as *Dear John.*
    Where should the salutation be placed?

4   Which comes first on an envelope?
    ☐   the first name
    ☐   the surname or family name

5   Where do we put the name of the letter-writer?

6   We usually end a letter with a complimentary close, such as *Yours sincerely.* Rank these closes from the most formal to the least formal.

    Yours
    Yours faithfully
    Yours truly
    Yours sincerely
    Love
    Yours ever

    Which one should you use if you began *Dear Sir/Madam*?
    Which ones could you use if you knew the reader well?

7   We often use a title before a person's name.
What do these titles mean?

Dr... Ms... Miss... Mr... Mrs... Prof...

8   Explain these conventions:

Robert Smith Esq
Messrs Smith and Jones

9   Explain the meaning of these abbreviations which are often used
in addresses.

plc,   Co.,   Ltd.,   Rd.,   Ave.,   St.,

2   Check your work

We should always check our business letters before we send them
out. This checklist can help.

A checklist for business correspondence

Have you written your name and address clearly?
Have you put the receiver's address?
Have you put any necessary reference numbers?
Have you included details of the advertisement or letter you are
    replying to?
Have you got the layout right?
Have you included an appropriate greeting?
Would it help the reader to put in an appropriate heading?
Did you start by telling the reader why you are writing?
Did you start with the most important point?
Did you keep the main points separate, by giving each main point its
    own paragraph or by using numbers, for example?
Have you asked for what you want?
Have you included any irrelevant information?
Have you checked the spelling, punctuation and grammar?
Does the letter have an appropriate and polite ending, such as
    I look forward to hearing from you?
Have you mentioned exactly what is enclosed?

If you are writing to complain about an item or a service check to see
that you have mentioned
• what the item or service is
• what has gone wrong with it
• when and where you bought it
• information about any previous letters or telephone calls, giving
  dates and times
• a specific request for action: for example, repair, replacement or
  your money back.

Task 1

Use the checklist on page 34 to find what is wrong with these letters.
Rewrite the letters when you have finished. Compare what you have
written in a small group.

Letter 1

26 Cam Court
Victoria Avenue
Cambridge
CB2 1EJ

12 July 1987

Advances Mail Order plc
FREEPOST
Market Street
Birmingham
B26 7BR

Dear Sir/Madam

I want to order the rocking chair in the advertisement and I
am enclosing a cheque.

I also want to know if you supply other furniture in a similar
style. Please send me your latest catalogue together with
details of prices.

I look forward to hearing from you.

P. Toms

Letter 2

52 Mount Helen
Kingston upon Thames
Surrey KT6 1QS

The Manager
Viking Washing Machines
Industrial Way
London E12 3DP

Dear Sir/Madam

I have now written to you twice but I have still received no answer. I
also telephoned your secretary last week and I was told there was no
trace of the letters. She suggested I ring the following day when you
or your deputy would be available. I spoke to Mr Adams and he said he
would send someone to look at my machine immediately. I am still
waiting.

I must say I am disappointed in your new product. I bought the machine
less than six months ago and it has been nothing but trouble. Last
week was the last straw. We plugged the machine in to do our weekly
washing and the plug exploded. It damaged my newly painted wall and
gave me and the cat a terrible fright. Please do something about the
problem, now!

Yours sincerely

G. Smith

G. Smith (Mr)

3 · Get a feel for style

When we are writing personal business letters it is important to use a formal style, but it is quite easy to use an old-fashioned style of English that complicates the message and makes the letter difficult to read.

Task 1

Read this letter carefully.

```
Dear Sir

I beg to acknowledge receipt of your letter of
the 15 inst. in connection with my not clearing
my account which was outstanding at the end of
June.

Please accept my profuse apologies.  We were
unable to settle this matter due to the fact
that I was overseas at the time, and as a
result was unable to act on your demand because
I did not receive it.  I have only just returned
and I am writing to you immediately with a
remittance of £350.

I hope that this delay did not inconvenience you,
nor lead you to believe that not paying my
balance on the date due, was in any way
intentional.

Yours faithfully
```

What is the writer trying to do? Discuss the function of the different sections of the letter.

Now complete this simpler version of the letter.

Dear Sir,

I am replying to . . . . . . asking me to . . . .

I apologize for not settling . . . ., but I did not . . . ., because . . . .

Please find enclosed . . . ., and accept my apologies . . . . . .

Yours faithfully,

It is possible to include all the information you need in a much simpler style. However, there is also a danger of being too informal. (See page 5 in Unit 1)

The most important characteristics of the style of a personal business letter are as follows:
- The language should be clear and give exact details: for example, write *the shoes I ordered on 12 July* rather than *the things I sent for.*
- The language should be brief and to the point. You should avoid extra information. (See letter 2 in Section 2 Task 1)
- You need to avoid using lengthy and old-fashioned expressions like *I beg to inform you.*
- You should also avoid using the sort of contractions we use in conversation: for example, you should write *I do not think it is right* rather than *I don't think it's right.*

One way to be brief and exact is to use the right words.

Task 2

Replace the following expressions in italics with words or expressions from the list below. Keep the same meaning.

1 *I think you ought to give me* a new one.
2 I am *really unhappy* with the cooker I bought.
3 Please send me a *new one.*
4 I would like *to have my money back.*
5 I want *some of my money back* because the hotel was nothing like the brochure.
6 I am sending you the ticket *that you asked me for* in your letter of 20 June 1987.

a refund	requested
I am entitled to	replacement
dissatisfied	compensation

Try to build up a list of similar expressions.

Task 3

We also need to control the language we use.

Look at the letter of complaint below. Certain sections of the text have been put into blocks and numbered. Complete this grid with the function of each of the numbered blocks. The first one has been done for you.

number	function
1	greeting
2	
3	
4	
5	
6	
7	

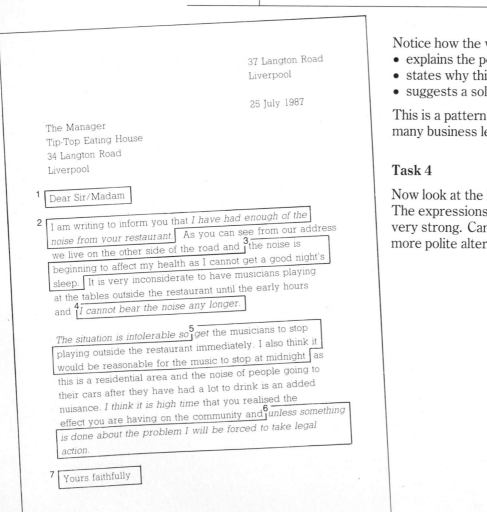

37 Langton Road
Liverpool

25 July 1987

The Manager
Tip-Top Eating House
34 Langton Road
Liverpool

1 Dear Sir/Madam

2 I am writing to inform you that *I have had enough of the noise from your restaurant.* As you can see from our address we live on the other side of the road and 3 the noise is beginning to affect my health as I cannot get a good night's sleep. It is very inconsiderate to have musicians playing at the tables outside the restaurant until the early hours and 4 *I cannot bear the noise any longer.*

The situation is intolerable so 5 get the musicians to stop playing outside the restaurant immediately. I also think it would be reasonable for the music to stop at midnight as this is a residential area and the noise of people going to their cars after they have had a lot to drink is an added nuisance. *I think it is high time* that you realised the effect you are having on the community and 6 *unless something is done about the problem I will be forced to take legal action.*

7 Yours faithfully

Peter Jones

Notice how the writer
- explains the position
- states why this is a problem
- suggests a solution.

This is a pattern you can use for many business letters.

Task 4

Now look at the letter again. The expressions in italics are very strong. Can you suggest more polite alternatives?

Task 5

Imagine you are the writer of the letter in Task 3. It has been two
weeks since you wrote the letter and you have had no reply. Write
and complain to the Managing Director of Tip-Top Eating Houses in
Britain. Write a letter that is calm and polite but make sure that your
reader knows about the problem and takes action.

Join a small group and discuss each of the letters with the help of the
checklist on page 34. Agree on one version and ask a member of your
group to read it to the class.

4   Building a list of expressions

You will be able to write better letters if you build up a collection of
suitable expressions. Add to this table when you get a chance. Some
expressions can be used in more than one type of letter.

type of letter	suitable openings	suitable endings
complaint	I am sorry to inform you	I look forward to hearing from you. I hope you can settle this matter to my satisfaction as soon as possible.
request for information	I would be grateful if you could send me . . . . . . In reply to your advertisement (give reference)	Thank you in anticipation. We look forward to receiving the information. I would be grateful if you could respond as soon as possible.
confirmation	Further to our conversation of (date), I am writing to confirm . . . . . . Thank you for your letter of (date). I would like to confirm	Thank you for your attention.

5 Structuring information

Here are some letters for you to write. Make sure that the information is in the most logical order!

Task 1

You have just been on an organized holiday with a group, and despite the advertisement the hotel you were staying in was very inadequate.

HOTEL REGAL CHRISTA

With beautiful luxurious gardens spread out over a large area, the Regal Christa justifiably boasts a splendidly relaxed setting. It stands ten minutes walk from the old town and about one and a half miles from the nearest beach, with marvellous views across the bay. Designed throughout in a traditional and rather elegant style, the hotel has earned an excellent reputation for comfort, friendly service and delicious food. If you want to take life easy, you'll enjoy stretching out on a sunbed by the pool. For the more active, there's tennis, table tennis and crazy-golf.

- swimming-pool with terrace
- beautiful gardens
- full air-conditioning
- attractive restaurant with excellent service
- two tennis courts; table tennis; crazy-golf
- TV and video
- dancing every night
- facilities for young children

You have made the following list of points to include in a letter of complaint.

no representative at the airport
left on July 21 and returned on 6 August
had to take a taxi to the hotel; cost equivalent of £14
dirty linen on the bed
lights not working in the rooms
very poor service in the restaurant
food was terrible
crockery not properly washed
swimming-pool was being repaired
the noise from the discothèque round the corner kept you awake
nothing like the brochure

Put these points (and any additional ones you think of) in the best order and write a letter of complaint to the tour operators. Remember to make your case and say what you want done: for example, a refund, compensation, etc.

Use the checklist on page 34 to check your first draft. Then rewrite the letter and discuss the final version in small groups.

Task 2

Imagine that you have just received the following letter.

Orion Hotels

26 Market Street   Oxford   OX1 2TP   Tel: 0865 223456

25 February 1987

Antoine Le Roux
30 Rue de Marrakech
Rabat
Morocco

Dear Mr Le Roux

Thank you for your letter of 20 February enquiring about the availability of a twin-bedded room with bath from 2 to 6 August 1987. I am sorry that all our rooms in that category will be occupied for that period as we are expecting a Conference Group. However, we can offer you a double room without a bath for that period if you so wish. Alternatively we would be pleased to receive you immediately before or after the dates in question.

Please let me have your reply as soon as possible.

Yours sincerely

Jane Smith

Jane Smith
Manager

Now draft your reply. Check your draft with the help of the checklist. Discuss your replies in small groups. Which is the most effective?

(If you are interested in further work on commercial correspondence you should consult *A Handbook of Commercial Correspondence* by A. Ashley, Oxford University Press.)

6

In my opinion

1 Introduction

Writing is often used to present an opinion. Some of the written media people use to express their opinions include books, letters to the press, personal and business correspondence, articles in newspapers and magazines, poems, etc. If these have not been available people have even taken to writing on walls!

As individuals trying to express yourselves in English, it is an advantage to be able to state your opinion in a clear and reasoned way, and the aim of this unit is to focus on how to do this.

2 Introducing the issue

When writing to express an opinion, the writer often begins by presenting or introducing the issue. This can be done in a variety of ways. For example, the writer may start by addressing the reader directly to get his or her sympathy. (See extract 1 on the next page.) The important thing is to attract the reader's attention while presenting the main point clearly and unambiguously.

Task 1

Read the following extracts. They are taken from the beginning of longer pieces which express an opinion.

Extract 1

You might think, as I once did, that only a madman or a fool would find himself in a position where, after 12 years of training and working 110 hours a week with poor financial rewards, he was still uncertain of getting a secure post in his chosen profession. Yet my husband and many other junior surgeons are in just that situation.

If the present government had . . . . . .

Extract 2

Last year the Third World owed Western banks over £1 trillion and paid more than £100 billion in interest. Every time the US banks raise their interest rates, thousands die in the Third World because money that should be used for food and health care is sent out to pay interest to foreign bankers. While their own people die of hunger, these poor countries are actually forced to export food so as to earn money to pay their debts. Brazil, the biggest debtor of all, owes £103 billion to these private bankers in New York and Frankfurt.

Extract 3

One man's holiday is another's peak workload. For the great majority of us to take our ease in the summer months, the minority have to work like blazes. Ferry crews, airline staff, waiters, porters, chambermaids, taxi drivers. Spare a thought for them as you stretch out under the sun. These are what the jargon calls service workers. They work in banks and building societies and hotels and restaurants and hairdressers. They don't make things, but they are indispensable to the world we live in, and there are more of them every year.

Yet service work does not have a high reputation. The British don't . . . . . .

Extract 4

How far should countries go in protecting their citizens against the adversities which may beset them? And how far should such protection be undertaken by their governments, and how far left to private agencies . . .? There has been in our own day a great revolution of thought on both of these issues. In one country after another, from the United States to the Soviet Union . . . . . .

Extract 5

In 1985, 5200 people died in UK road accidents. Reliable sources estimate that nearly 3000 of the deaths were caused by drunken or otherwise irresponsible driving. Yet while the majority of killer motorists receive lenient sentences, the lives of their victims and relatives are shattered.

Discuss the extracts in pairs and complete the following grid. What
do you think the main topic is in each case? How is it introduced? The
first example has been done for you.

Extract	Topic	How it is introduced
1	Working conditions for junior surgeons	A direct address to the reader to get sympathy and outline problem
2		
3		
4		
5		

Note how 'yet' is used in extracts 3 and 5 to signal the surprising
nature of what is being said in view of what was said in the section
before. This is a useful device for introducing an issue.

Task 2

Look at these photographs illustrating some social problems. Write
the introduction to an essay in which you will try to persuade your
colleagues to accept your opinion about one of the problems.
Experiment with the techniques you looked at in the previous task.

Task 3

In small groups discuss the introductions you wrote.

Do the opening sentences make you want to read the rest?
Is the issue clearly presented?

3   Presenting your arguments

Once you have attracted the reader's attention, the next stage is to
present your arguments. Some of the ways you might do this include:
- putting forward arguments (and counter arguments) which may
  include facts and figures without using the first person.

For example: Evidence from abroad indicates that the introduction of
imprisonment for all those convicted of drinking and driving does
have a deterrent effect. But once drink-drive offenders realize the
chances of being caught are slim, alcohol related road accidents
increase.

Another possibility is to attribute the arguments to someone else by
using expressions such as *They say that* . . . or *People who believe in
nuclear power argue that* . . . . This may be combined with personal
opinion or not.

- a statement of your personal opinions which is clearly marked as
  such by the use of *I* or *In my opinion,* etc.

For example: I am sure that the government could find a more
acceptable solution to the problem if . . .

- a direct appeal to the reader.

For example: If you are lucky, it may even work. The final insult is that you will probably have to pay for the privilege of using such facilities. So why don't we complain more . . .?

Make sure your argument is clear! Use linkers like *yet, if, so* and *but*, and arrange the information in a logical way.

Task 1

It is possible to connect your argument by using questions which are asked for effect rather than information. In these extracts the question is missing. Try and replace it.

1   Issues affecting women are seen as fringe matters, although women make up 51 per cent of the population.
    . . . . ? In the US, women have been organizing their votes to make sure that the politicians have to take notice of them.

2   The Chernobyl accident was a disaster for the Ukraine but not a total disaster for Russia. Thousands of hectares of agricultural land will be unusable for the foreseeable future. But the Ukraine is vast. Russia is vast. The USSR can survive the loss of a slice of its agricultural land. It is a major inconvenience, not a major disaster.

    . . . . ? Some of our reactors are situated in very densely populated areas. If it were necessary to evacuate people from a 10-mile area around the Hartlepool reactor it would mean moving nearly half a million people from their homes.

Task 2

The expressions which help to outline the argument in this text are missing. Replace them with the help of the words and expressions in the list at the bottom. Some of the choices may be inappropriate. Check your answers with a partner.

Rather than exploiting the environment, shouldn't we be in partnership? . . . . we continue to waste the earth's resources as if there were no tomorrow, there could well be no tomorrow.

. . . . the year 2000, one third of the world's cropland will have turned to dust. One million species will have become extinct and hundreds of millions of people will face starvation. All this is happening . . . . our civilization has kept on expanding, on the assumption that the world's resources are limitless. . . . . merely stopping growth is not the answer. . . . . we need is development that works in partnership with the environment, that uses the earth's resources more productively and . . . . at the same time is sustainable. This is . . . . *Earthlife* exists. At the moment our approach is unique among conservation groups. . . . . the business community is the sector of society which has the greatest influence on our future, we're aiming to change the way it thinks and operates. We want it to accept conservation as an integral principle of economic development. We're trying to do this by working together with governments, businesses and international agencies to show that conservation can be commercially successful.

. . . ., if it's commercially successful how can the business community afford to ignore it?

after   what   if   because   but   since   by
after all   yet   consequently   the reason   actually

Task 3

In Britain there is growing controversy about the use of live animals for experiments. This use of animals is known as vivisection. The arguments can be passionate. A group known as the Animal Liberation Front has released animals in attacks on research stations, and some members even advocate violence against scientists involved in these tests.

Imagine you are a journalist. Write a short piece asking your readers what they think of the issue. Use the arguments in the table below.

for	*against*
Animal tests are essential. Without them drugs like insulin would not be developed.	Animals are not only used for medical reasons, but also for cosmetics.
Future tests are needed to cure cancer and epilepsy, for example.	Animals are used for chemical warfare tests.
Cosmetic tests make sure beauty products don't cause cancer.	Failure of drugs like thalidomide show animals are not a realistic guide to human reaction.
Animals used are mainly specially bred rats and mice.	The experiments are very cruel.

Your article should follow this structure:

paragraph 1 Present the issue.
paragraph 2 Outline the arguments for vivisection without using the first person.
paragraph 3 Outline the arguments against vivisection without using the first person.

Conclude the piece by asking readers for their opinion.

Compare what you have written in small groups.

4   Coming to a conclusion

In a good piece of writing the ideas and arguments in the preceding paragraphs should lead to an appropriate conclusion. The writer has the option of making a request or a demand for action but in any case the end should be obvious to the reader.

Task 1

The paragraphs of the text below have been put in the wrong order. Try to rearrange the text back into the right order. In doing this decide which of the paragraphs serve to
- introduce the problem
- outline the arguments
- bring the arguments to a conclusion.

1   Admittedly, there have been some attempts at improvement. The new space age superloos are unisex (10 pence to all) and more hygienic as they're completely cleaned after each use. Yet they have drawbacks. Often situated in highly visible spots, thus maximising self-consciousness, they also have automatic doors which you fear may either whizz open too early and expose you to the crowds, or never open at all, leaving you a prisoner. Not ideal.

2   Reason tells me that I can't be the only one. Other women, too, must have stood in line, cursing the fact that yet again there is only one ladies' lavatory in a crowded pub. Friendships can be formed in the time you spend waiting.

3   So why don't we complain more about our toilets? Perhaps it's embarrassment about raising such a 'delicate' subject in public. It's time to campaign for public conveniences to be more available, clearly signposted, regularly maintained, free and clean. Make your feelings known by complaining to the local Cleansing department who should be in the telephone directory listed under your local council.

4   And I can't be the only woman who resolutely avoids public conveniences and goes out of her way to head for the department store where the ladies' will be clean, free and easy to find.

5   Lack of provision of ladies' loos isn't the only problem. Even if you are lucky enough to find public toilets where the council hides them, they are often so dirty and smelly that only sheer desperation could drive you to use them. The walls may be covered in graffiti, locks broken, floors wet and muddy, basins encrusted with grime. The taps (cold water only) may well be dripping into a pool of scummy water above the clogged-up plughole and you won't see anything of such luxuries as toilet paper, soap or towels. There may, ironically, be a 'hygienic' air hand dryer — and if you're lucky, it may even work. The final insult is that you will probably have to pay for the privilege of using such facilities.

6 If only there were more lavatory attendants like Reg Bedwell (pictured above), who looks after Covent Garden's loos. He ensures that they always have flowers, nice soap, clean towels and even music. He keeps the place spotless. What a hero!

Task 2

In Britain more and more restaurants are introducing 'no smoking' zones.

People sometimes express their opinions on issues like this in letters to the editor. Read these extracts from two letters responding to an article in a newspaper. The conclusions are missing. Write an appropriate conclusion for each letter.

Letter 1

I was disappointed to read that your food editor (*Viewpoints*, last week) thinks that restaurant managers who want to introduce non-smoking tables are 'do-gooders and spoil-sports'.

Doesn't he know that the majority of people in this country do not smoke? In a survey carried out in 1983, 79% of non-smokers, 71% of ex-smokers, and 43% of smokers said they would like a ban on smoking in restaurants.

Letter 2

It is about time someone spoke up against smoking bans and I very much agree with your food editor's views on this 'intolerable imposition' in an increasing number of restaurants in Britain.

I do enjoy occasionally smoking after a meal, and would strongly object to being told whether I can smoke or not. If restaurants have an efficient air-conditioning system, I cannot see that smokers would disturb anyone else.

Read the conclusions you have written to the other members of the class.

Are they all the same or different? Discuss the functions of the different conclusions you came to.

5   Presenting your point of view

This photograph was taken in a government office in London, but bureaucracy affects all of us!

Task 1

Work with a partner and exchange your experiences of bureaucracies. Have you ever had problems applying for a passport or visa, for example?

Tell each other your stories and list the specific problems of the system you encountered.

Now join a small group and compare your lists. Are there any points that you particularly agree or disagree with?

Find solutions to as many of the problems as possible. Make notes of the solutions you find interesting, for the next task.

Task 2

Imagine that you have been asked to write a 150 word article for a local newspaper. The purpose of the article is to give your opinion on how to improve an area of bureaucracy that you feel strongly about. Follow this procedure:

Before you write
Refer to your previous discussion and choose an area that you feel strongly about. Make notes under the following headings:
• Examples of the problem
• Negative effects of the problem
• Solutions

While you write

Introduce the problem through a series of examples. You may wish to get the reader on your side with a direct appeal, such as *Have you ever . . . . . .* or *Don't you find that . . . . . .* or *One of our main problems when we . . . . . .*

Tell the reader why you think it is a problem.

Outline a solution (or solutions) to the problem. Remember to give reasons.

Now work with a partner. Look through your first drafts and discuss these questions:

- Is the argument clear and logical? Why? Give examples.
- Are there any sections that distract or confuse the reader? How? Give examples.
- Did you state facts (and figures), give your personal opinion or use a mixture of these? Make sure that the point of view is consistent.
- Was the solution clearly presented? Did the examples lead naturally to the solution? How?
- Was the spelling, grammar and use of linkers appropriate?

Rewrite your article in the light of the comments above.

6   Achieving a sense of balance

We are sometimes required to present both sides of an argument (even if we don't always agree with the other side). We usually do this in order to present a balanced picture because it is quite effective to show that you are aware of all the arguments in coming to a conclusion.

Look back at Section 3 Task 3 before starting.

Task 1

Arguments for nuclear power

1   The demand for energy is increasing but our resources of the fossil fuels — gas, coal and oil — are fixed and they are decreasing all the time.
2   Nuclear energy is a way of conserving these fuels and generating electricity less expensively.
3   There is no practical alternative to petrol and diesel for road transport, so it is sensible to conserve them. Coal can be used to manufacture plastics and pharmaceuticals. Uranium, which is used to generate nuclear electricity, has no other significant commercial use.
4   Nuclear power is clean and cheap. Nuclear power stations are cheaper to run than conventional power stations.
5   There is very little pollution from nuclear power. Nuclear fuel can be reprocessed and reused and the waste carefully stored or disposed of according to stringent international regulations.

6   Radioactive material from nuclear power is a very small proportion of the radioactive materials in our environment.

7   Nuclear plants are designed with safety in mind, and the environment, the workplace and the employees are carefully monitored.

Look at the list of arguments above outlining the case for nuclear power. Work with a partner and think of the arguments against. Compare your list with the other students so that you build up your own list of counter arguments.

Now work individually and write a 150 word essay on the advantages and disadvantages of nuclear power. In doing this you should

- introduce the topic by giving your reader reasons for looking at the problem at this time.
- go through the arguments for and against. Group similar arguments together. You may find the following linkers helpful: *however, in contrast, while, besides, for example, such as.*
- present all the arguments but in doing so you should lead to a conclusion, which may be

    ☐   for nuclear power

    ☐   against nuclear power

    ☐   that further evidence is required.

1 Introduction

Task 1

Here are extracts from three descriptions of the same property. The aim of each one is to tell the reader where it is located. Read them and then answer the questions below.

Extract 1
The Grange is a small select development set in the centre of the charming village of Blackstock.

The development comprises eight carefully positioned and skilfully designed dwellings in large attractive plots. The accommodation provides four and five bedroomed detached homes of one or two storeys, fitted to the highest standard and specification.

Blackstock is a delightful village about five miles south east of the city of Oxford. The village has a primary school and other excellent facilities including a supermarket, chemist, bakers and inns. The nearby university city of Oxford has good shopping and schooling facilities.

Extract 2
This property forms part of a small new development of houses and bungalows being constructed by Lockton Estates Group. Plot 5 is a similar size to Plot 6, the other properties being smaller. Blackstock is a pleasant village offering all the usual amenities and located about four miles from Oxford city centre.

Extract 3
Blackstock is about four miles from the centre of Oxford and there has been a lot of development there recently. However, The Grange is in a quiet cul-de-sac which is only a few minutes walk from the centre of the village which boasts among other things an excellent pub and Chinese take-away. Shopping is very convenient but it is very quiet and often the only sound we can hear is the chiming of the church clock...

Which description is taken from
- a personal letter?
- the builder's publicity?
- a report on the property?

Give reasons for your answers.

When we are writing we sometimes need to provide a description. The sort of description we provide will of course depend on our purpose. In the examples above the builder is keen to emphasize facts that may influence people to buy the properties. Consequently we find expressions like 'carefully positioned' and 'skilfully designed'. The report aims to be short and to the point, while the writer of the personal letter can select facts likely to be of interest to the reader. Each writer has had to decide on which aspects to include or ignore as well as the amount of detail which needs to be provided for the reader. This unit concentrates on ways in which we can select and organize the language we need for description.

2 Selecting a viewpoint

When we are writing a description we have to decide on our point of view. Are we being positive or negative? Are we describing what we're looking at from a general point of view or are we concerned with detail?

Task 1

Look at this photograph of an alley-way. Imagine that you were present when the photograph was taken. Make a list of
- the things you saw
- the sounds you might have heard
- the smells
- the colours
- the tastes.

Build the words in your list up into groups of adverbs and adjectives to form phrases like

a very old alley-way
an open dustbin
the sound of children.

Compare your list and phrases in a small group. Did you react in the same way? Discuss why you chose particular words.

3   Creating a mood

As we saw in Section 2 Task 1, our choice of adjectives helps to
capture what we feel about a place.

Task 1

The material in this section comes from an advertisement entitled
Brilliant Thailand. Part of the text reads 'And wherever you go
throughout the Kingdom you will be surrounded by a brilliant blaze of
colour'.
Insert the colour words from the list below into these sentences from
the advertisement.

The glowing . . . . of temples and palaces.

The sun-drenched . . . . of cloudless skies.

The . . . . and . . . . of exotic orchids.

The hot . . . . chillies at a floating market.

The . . . . and . . . . of iridescent coral
seas.

The . . . . jungle and rice fields.

blue   gold   purples   red   turquoise   aquamarines
emerald green   pinks

Write similar expressions that represent what you feel about the
town you are living in
- on a sunny day when you are feeling bright and cheerful
- on a rainy day when you are feeling miserable.

Read what you have written to the other students and make a note of
the best examples.

Task 2

Look at this poem. The writer is describing a scene which is similar to the one in the photograph in Section 2 Task 1. Some of the adjectives are missing. Fill the gaps with adjectives that capture the mood of decay.

The Old Alley

. . . . papers cling to . . . . stone,

Dustbin lids rock to and fro in the . . . . wind,

Milk cartons, beer bottles and newspapers

Squeeze through holed, rusty and . . . . bins.

. . . . drainpipes hang from . . . . and

    depressing walls,

Thieving rats raid . . . . houses.

A . . . . smell reeks from open drains,

. . . . windows reveal . . . . and musty

    places behind.

Shadows hang dolefully on . . . . brick,

The echoes of children playing bounces back off

Each alley wall.

A . . . . dog limps in the gutter,

Sniffing at the drains — whining for food.

From a poem by Richard Partridge

Discuss your choice of adjectives before looking at the key.

4   Our view of people

The way we describe a person will depend on why we are doing it. When we are producing a description for an official purpose, such as for the police, we need to include a lot of factual information about the person's age, height, weight, etc. In a letter or piece of creative writing we select what we include to create an impression of the person. One way we can do this is to 'paint a picture' of the actions which are characteristic of the person: for example, 'My father used to sit cracking his knuckles' rather than 'My father had nervous habits'.

Task 1

Complete this checklist of the points we might include when we describe a person.

age   height   size   personality   . . . .

. . . .

Task 2

Read the following description of a character in *A Rose for Winter* by
Laurie Lee. In it Lee describes his first meeting with one of the
residents of a small Spanish fishing village.

Sitting one morning outside a sea-front cafe, eating cooked liver and
drinking the golden wine, we caught sight of a striking figure advancing
up the street towards us. He was a tall man, wide hipped and narrow
shouldered, shaped like a sherry cask, and on the top of his head he
wore a black beret hardly bigger than a button. But what particularly
drew one's attention was not so much his size as his booming voice and
the extravagant, almost royal gestures with which he saluted everyone in
his path. To each of these, man, woman, child and dog, he bellowed
greetings as he came, and his face was lit by a vast and insane smile.
Loose-lipped and flabby-handed, rolling and posturing on his tiny feet, he
looked a terror. 'Watch him', we said, as he approached. He caught our
eye, stopped dead, spun his great bulk on the point of his shoes, swept
off his hat, and bowed. 'Distinguished visitors!' he boomed. 'Welcome to
Castillo. Do you wish to pass a pleasant hour? Honour me then with your
company and I will show you my beautiful farm.'

What impression do you have of the man? (How old do you think he
is? Is he big or small? etc.) Underline the expressions that
• describe the man's physical appearance
• describe the man's actions and gestures.

Go through the checklist in Task 1 and in pairs discuss what you think
the man looks like. Are you able to imagine detail which is not
supplied in the text? Why?

Imagine the man in the description is missing. How would you
describe him to the police?

Task 3

Look back at the expressions that describe the man in the text in
Task 2. Notice how Laurie Lee uses adjectives to give the reader
further information about the physical characteristics of the person he
is describing: for example, the man is *wide* hipped, has a *booming*
voice, etc.

All the adjectives in the list below might be used in physical
description. Use them to build up a list of expressions like
'a squeaky voice', 'a soft pair of hands' and so on.

*squeaky   soft   high-pitched   round   protruding   gentle   slender
powerful   tight   flowing   bare   curly   delicate   serious   timid
narrow   flat   arched   weak*

Read your expressions to the other students and build up a list you
can use in future.

Task 4

Imagine you have to write a short description of an elderly relative. Start by making a list of
• the person's main physical characteristics
• some of the actions which are characteristic of this person.

Write a description which is similar to the one in the text in Task 2.

Exchange descriptions in small groups and decide on the most effective description. Identify the words and phrases which bring the person to life.

5   People and places

When we want to describe a place we have been to it is sometimes useful to emphasize our feelings by including a description of the people there and what they were doing.

Task 1

Look at this photograph of the *Yeni Cami*, or New Mosque, from across the Golden Horn in Istanbul.

Imagine you are standing where the photograph was taken. What can you see? What sounds and smells would you expect? Who are the people in the photograph? What are they doing?

Discuss your thoughts in a small group and compare them to these short extracts about the area from a guide to Istanbul.

These little boats churn the foul waters of the Golden Horn into a phosphorescent spectrum of greens and blues.

Old men stare at boats which have probably not changed since the days of Byzantium.

The wooden ships and scows transport much of the produce for the fruit and vegetable markets on the shore of the Golden Horn.

The whole area is dominated by the imposing mass of Yeni Cami, built in the seventeenth century.

The silhouette is a graceful, flowing curve from one dome to another.

The two minarets have balconies.

Were you able to build up a picture of the area from the photograph alone or did you need the additional information? Did your knowledge of the world help?

Task 2

You are writing a letter to a friend who has never been to Turkey. Complete this account of your walk in the area opposite the *Yeni Cami*. Try to share your mood and feelings with your friend. Use the material you looked at and discussed in Task 1 but add any details you want. Aim to write about seventy words.

Remember that qualifying every noun with an adjective doesn't make a good description. We have to choose our adjectives carefully so that they all help to create the mood.

Begin *I've been in Istanbul for almost a week now. This morning I went for a walk by the Golden Horn. . . . . .*

Work in a small group. Read what each of you has written and decide how effectively you have conveyed your mood. Tell each other which words and phrases are most effective.

Task 3

Imagine that you were present at this event. Write down ten adjectives or phrases that you feel capture the colour and excitement of the event.

Form a group of four or five students and agree on a list of fifteen expressions. Work as a group and use the expressions you have chosen to write one paragraph of a magazine article.

Exchange your descriptions with the other groups.

In what way are the descriptions similar or different?
Did you choose the same words or create the same mood?
Make a note of any interesting alternative expressions.

Task 4

Think of a place that you remember from the past: a town or a house, for example. Imagine that you are famous and you have to write a 150 word description for a magazine article entitled *A place I remember*. Make notes for the article under the following headings:

Introduction
Why is the place important to you? When were you there? What emotions do you feel when you think of this place? Are you happy, sad or nostalgic?

Main section
What are the things that you remember? Are there any people or animals who were part of the place? What were they like? What actions were characteristic of them?

Conclusion
What does the place mean to you today? Do you ever go back? Why? Why not?

Make sure that you paint an interesting picture by capturing the mood of the place.

1 Introduction

We do a lot of writing for external reasons. We may write to get
things done, to communicate our ideas and feelings to a friend, or to
pass an exam, for example. Very few of us have the need to write
poems or stories (even in our own language) and yet creative writing
can be a source of pleasure as well as language improvement. The
purpose of this unit is to suggest ways in which you might start to
write for and about yourself in English.

2 Building a personal album

In the past, personal albums which contained a mixture of drawings,
sayings, poems, jokes, etc., were very common. The idea was that
the owner or a friend would start the album and anyone who looked
at it would contribute to it.

Task 1

Look at these extracts from an old album. Discuss each of them and
decide on what they mean.

Me, myself, I

All the entries were written in the 1920s so the humour is a little
dated. As you can see the contributions don't need to be original but
they should mean something to you.

Task 2   (Done outside class)

Start by building up a collection of material around themes such as friendship, farewells, dreams and memories. The material may consist of jokes, poems, sayings, cartoons and so on, and sources might include collections of poems, magazines, books, etc.

Buy a small album or exercise book with plain paper.

Task 3

Form a small group with students that you know quite well. Read the material you have collected to each other. Talk about the pieces that you like and dislike and ask members of the group to put something in your album. When they have finished you can pass the album to other members of the class. Anyone who reads it however, must provide additional material.

3   Keeping a diary

A diary is a journal or record of events. It can take many forms: some diaries are very personal while others may be quite public, and in English we use the same word to refer to a calendar where we keep a record of forthcoming appointments.

Task 1

In this task we will aim to discuss diaries. As an introduction, start by completing the survey below. You may have to move around the classroom.

Find someone in the class who

		Name
1	keeps a diary of forthcoming events in his/her pocket or handbag	. . . .
2	keeps a desk diary	. . . .
3	keeps a record of things that happened during the day	. . . .
4	keeps old diaries and reads them again occasionally	. . . .
5	has read the published diary of a famous person	. . . .
6	keeps a diary of special occasions such as weddings	. . . .
7	used to keep a diary but no longer does so	. . . .
8	has kept a diary for research purposes	. . . .

Now discuss these questions.

Why do people keep diaries?
What sort of information do people include in diaries?
What sort of information do people leave out of diaries?
Are any diaries part of the literature of your country? Tell the other
    students what you know about them.

Task 2

Diaries are more than a catalogue of dates and events. Look at the
following extracts from some diaries and answer the questions below
each one.

Extract 1
Saturday 19 March
I have received a reply to my letter to the Prime Minister from somebody
called S.M. Williams. It is very short and to the point, and enclosed with it
is a list of arms control negotiations in which Britain is involved. I must
say that with all these negotiations taking place I am surprised no
progress has yet been made. I showed this list to Roger, who complained
that it does not include our own overtures to Mr Andropov. I pointed
out that it was prepared before the government was aware of our
involvement, and that doubtless our modest efforts would be included in
the reprint.

1   What does 'it' in the second sentence refer to?
2   What do you think the 'overtures to Mr Andropov' were about?
3   What is the diary about?
4   What can you say about the subject of most of the sentences?

Extract 2
It was the evening of the 16th June, 1862; the largest stars were already
visible in the blue depths of a cloudless sky, while the crescent moon,
high to the west, shone as she shines in those heavens, and promised us
assistance for some hours of our night march . . . Behind us lay in a mass
of dark outline, the walls and castle of Maan, its houses and gardens, and
further back in the distance the high and barren range of the Sheraa
mountains merging into the coast chain of the Hejaz. Before and behind
us extended a wide and level plain . . . . . .

1   The writer was W. M. Palgrave who was a famous explorer of
    Arabia. Underline all the adjectives he uses. Why are there so
    many? What is he trying to achieve?
2   Why does he use 'us'?

Extract 3
February 4th, Yonda
A bad night. I could find no comfortable position on the hard mattress: a
touch of rheumatism from the sweat: mosquitoes droning outside my
meat-cover. Woke at six-forty to an overcast morning. Wrote to my

mother and then took Julian Green's journal down to the Congo and found a place to read free from ants on board the rusty metal boat. Always astonished at the procession of grassy islands endlessly in progress at four miles an hour out of the heart of Africa, none, however small, overtaking another.

Graham Greene is one of the most well-known modern English authors. In 1959 he went to Africa to research a novel. The extract above is from a record of his visit.

1 Underline all the verbs in the extract. Which of the verbs do not have a subject?
2 Why was it 'a bad night'? How does Greene use a minimum of words to describe it?
3 What impressions do you get of Africa from this short extract? What language does he use to achieve these impressions?

As you can see we can use diaries for a variety of purposes. We may want to
• tell the story of a personal campaign or crusade
• describe exactly what we have seen
• use the diary to record any thoughts, feelings or actions that are particularly memorable at the time. As Greene said 'I took the advantage to talk aloud to myself.'
Some diaries are written in 'diary style' with the omission of the subject and the verb 'to be'. Others are strong first person narratives. The style we use may well depend on our reason for keeping the diary.

4 Some diary projects

Although it is more natural to keep a diary in your mother tongue,
choose one of the following diary projects to help you with your
language learning.

Task 1 In my experience

The aim of this project is to 'talk aloud to yourself' about new
experiences and would be most appropriate when you are away from
home. Follow this procedure for about one week:

1 Set aside about ten minutes at the end of each day for writing
   your diary.
2 Start by making notes of anything memorable. This may be one or
   two words.
       For example: Went to Ely cathedral; met a policeman, etc.
3 Go through the notes and see if you can identify exactly what it is
   you remember. Try to add adjectives or images which capture
   what you saw or felt.
       For example: Went to Ely cathedral. The afternoon light which
       came in through the stained-glass windows was fantastic. An
       organ played while choir boys in red and white . . . . . .
   Use a dictionary to find the words you need.
4 If you want to, share your diary with a friend or your teacher.

Task 2 Diary of an extra-terrestrial

Imagine that you are an extra-terrestrial (E.T.) who has come to the
country you live in. As E.T. you are invisible and have decided to
keep a diary about the habits of people in your country.

1 Set aside about ten minutes a day for a period of a week.
2 Make a note of all your activities for the day.
3 Now go through your list and choose a few that would seem
   strange to a person from outside your culture or society.
4 Write a description of what you saw from the point of view of
   E.T. So an E.T. in England might write the following account
   about English tea.

   I had a cup of tea today. The English make tea in a strange way. They
   boil water in a cooking implement called a kettle. When the water
   boils they add it to some leaves in a tea pot. They then pour it into a
   tea cup and add milk and sugar!

5 At the end of you project you should exchange diaries with other
   E.T.s.

5   Writing poetry

Many of us have never written a poem in our own language, so why
should we try to write a poem in a foreign language?
Here are some good reasons why:

- Poetry requires us to express our feelings and ideas. To do this we
  need to use all the language we know and this is a way of extending
  our competence.
- Writing poetry gives us a chance to use language in different ways;
  to give new meanings to familiar words, and to develop a feel for
  the language.

How should you start?

The easiest way is to start by reading lots of English poetry so that
you get an idea of the types of poetry available. You can then start by
imitating the form and style of poets that you like. The tasks in this
section will give you some idea of how to continue and you might also
be interested in *Poem into Poem* by Alan Maley and Sandra Moulding.

Task 1

The poet Adrian Henri has published a collection of poems which try
to recreate his childhood and adolescence. The collection is entitled
Autobiography, and it covers the period from 1932 to 1964 and 1970.
Start by reading the openings below of three of the major sections.

Part One 1932–51
I
flags and bright funnels of ships
walking with my mother over the Seven Bridges
and being carried home too tired
frightened of the siren on the ferryboat
or running down the platform on the Underground   5
being taken over the river to see the big shops at Christmas
the road up the hill from the noisy dockyard
and the nasty smell from the tannery you didn't like going past
steep road that made your legs tired . . . . . .

Part Two 1951–57
I
young
art student
under the bridges of Paris
(where else)
painting badlypainted picturepostcard paintings   5
Pont des Arts, St-Germain-l'Auxerrois
sketchbook
corduroy elbows on the pernod table

Part Three 1957–64

I
warm diagonal red-and black-tiles
fire burning in the deep chimneyplace
whitepainted wooden rockingchair white walls
big regency-striped settee
winter in the little basement yard outside   5
her voice singing high piping in the kitchen
Saturdaymorning nowork breakfast
reading the *New Statesman*
flames echoing on the low white ceiling   9

Which period of the poet's life is each section about?

The poet tries to build an impression of himself and his life through a series of images. Let's look at how he does it.

Look at Part 1 again.

The poet is recording his memories. Expand this section by using verbs like 'I remember'. What exactly does he remember?

Look at the adjectives he uses. Are they positive or negative? How would you describe this period of his life?

Look at Part 2 again.

In this section the poet is describing himself. What was he doing in that period of his life? Was he successful?

What photograph would capture the image of 'corduroy elbows on a pernod table'?

Look at Part 3 again.

In the first four lines the poet is describing how a room was decorated.
He does this by adding adjectives to each of the nouns. Expand each of the noun groups in the following way:

The walls were white.
The tiles were : . . . . . .

Expand lines 7 to 9 into normal sentences. Start with *It was . . .*
What parts of speech has the poet left out?

Task 2

The poet writes that he used old photographs, letters and notebooks to help create the words and images in the poem. Choose one or more periods of your life and try to do the same.

Use Henri's technique to build up a poem of your own. For example, you might begin with:

young
language student
under the spires of Oxford
(where else)

Read your poems to each other in small groups.

6   Starting to write haiku

On a withered branch
  a crow has settled...
    autumn nightfall.

from the Japanese by Basho

Haiku is a form of poetry the Japanese have practised for centuries. Classical Japanese haiku are constructed according to rules which are often discussed and interpreted but rarely broken. The rules are as follows:

1   A haiku usually has seventeen Japanese syllables.
2   A haiku contains at least some reference to nature, (not human nature).
3   It refers to a specific event: it is not a generalization.
4   It presents the event as happening now, not in the past.

The form has been adapted to English as these examples show.

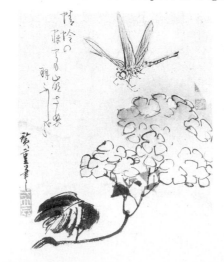

A bitter morning:
  Sparrows sitting together
    Without any necks.

Sunset: carrying
  a red balloon, he looks back...
    a child leaves the zoo.

The town clock's face
  adds another shade of yellow
    to the afterglow.

Lily
  out of the water
  out of itself

Task 1

Read the haiku on page 68, which were written in English, and then answer these questions.

1 Haiku in English have three lines. Many of them have five syllables in the first line, seven in the second and five in the third. Do these examples follow the rules?
2 What aspect of nature does each example portray? For example, what is the season in the first haiku?
3 What is the event suggested by each of the haiku?
4 What is the emotion connected with the event?

Task 2

The discipline required for haiku will help you to write better. Follow these simple instructions for writing a haiku of your own.

The simplest form of haiku is a description of an event that arouses an emotion, like these examples:

Gold, brown, and red leaves
    All twirling and scattering
        As the children play.

Squatting motionless
    the suntanned child and the toad
        stare at each other.

Choose a simple event and see if you can write a haiku around it.

Read your poem silently and make sure
• you try to follow the 5–7–5 rule as closely as possible
• it sounds right
• it refers to nature
• it is simple and yet full of emotion.

Show your haiku to each other and work at improving them.

Here is a hint: if you are working on a particular theme or area, it helps to make a note of all the ideas which you normally associate with that theme. So for 'apple' we might think of blossom, appletart, autumn, sauce, etc. Building up associations will help us create the images we need for this form of writing.

9

Anything to report?

1 Introduction

For some of us writing a report is part of our daily lives.

Task 1

Get into small groups and find someone who has experience of writing one or more of the following types of reports in English or their own language.

1 A report which describes the progress being made in carrying out a project or planned work.
2 A report on a scientific experiment.
3 A record of what happened at a meeting (i.e., the minutes).
4 A critical review of an event (e.g., a course of study).
5 A planning report which describes the results of a comparison between a number of alternatives (e.g., which equipment to buy).
6 An insurance report (e.g., a report of an accident).

Discuss what information you would expect in each type of report.

Task 2

As we saw on pages 6 and 7 of Unit 1, the use of titles and headings helps to make reports easier to read. Here are some standard headings we might use with various reports.

Conclusions
Aim
Methods of investigation
Introduction
Recommendations
Results
Findings

Discuss these questions.

1 Decide on the meaning of each of the headings.
2 Would any of these headings be used in the types of report listed in Task 1? Which headings go with which report?
3 What order would you expect the headings to appear in?

Headings are just one of the conventions of report writing. In this unit you will get practice in the way we approach report writing in English.

2   How did it happen?

We sometimes need to explain the cause of an accident for insurance purposes.

Task 1

Read these extracts from letters to an insurance company. Insert appropriate expressions in the gaps.

Extract 1

I *was walking* along Moore Rd. at 9.30 p.m. It *was* very dark . . . . the streetlights *were not working*. I walked into a large rock and bruised my toe. I needed medical treatment and . . . . I was unable to work for a week. I am . . . . writing to claim:

1   My medical expenses (receipt enclosed)
2   Compensation for loss of earnings during the period 21.3.87 to 28.3.87 (statement of earnings enclosed)

Extract 2

I am writing to report the theft of an Olympus OM 2 camera from our hotel room. The theft occurred . . . . my wife and I *were relaxing* by the pool on 28 June 1987. . . . . the doors to the window and room *were locked* the thief managed to get in by asking the hotel reception for a key. The theft was reported to the police and . . . . . .

Look at the tense forms in italics.
• What tense is being used?
• Can you describe how this tense works?

Make sure that you understand how this form is used in this type of writing.

Task 2

Work with a partner. Look at the photograph of the accident. What do you think happened? Select one statement from each group below to help you provide an explanation.

Group A

The roads were wet and slippery.
The sun was in the eyes of one of the drivers.
Visibility was very bad because of heavy rain.

Group B

The traffic lights were not working properly.
The brakes failed in one of the cars.
The engine suddenly stopped just before the road junction.

Group C

Both of the drivers were travelling above the speed limit.
One of the drivers was speeding.
Both of the drivers were driving normally.

Task 3

DESCRIPTION OF ACCIDENT (If necessary, please use the back of this form to provide full information)
Please state how accident happened and draw a diagram showing the width of the road, position of the vehicles involved and the direction in which originally proceeding. Comment where appropriate on speed and weather conditions.

BLAME (Put 'x' in appropriate box)

Self	
Other Party	
Both	

Date ....
Signature
Driver ....
(where other than Policyholder)

Signature
Policyholder ....
(if Company add Rubber Stamp or state position held)

MC2 (PD 09/84 — 200M)   Registered in Scotland No 2116. Registered Office: Pitheavlis, Perth, Scotland PH2 0NH

Continue working in pairs. Each of you should complete this section of a motor accident report form from the point of view of one of the drivers. You must both stick to the facts you have agreed on in Task 2 but you can add additional information. Follow the instructions carefully. Start with *I was travelling* . . . . . .

Your aim is to
• give the insurance company a clear description of the accident
• put at least some of the blame on the other party.

Task 4

Form a small group of six to eight students. Look at the descriptions written by each of the pairs with the help of this checklist.

- Is the description clear and easy to follow?
- Is the information logically presented?
- Is the use of tenses appropriate?
- Does the writer succeed in blaming the other party?

Suggest ways of improving the reports if the answer to any of these questions is 'no'.

3   Some characteristics of reports

In general the reason for writing a report should be stated in the introduction.
For example:

Introduction
The purpose of this report is to advise the office manager on the purchase of filing cabinets. We looked at three different cabinets and we will discuss the merits of each one.

Reports must be clear and the headings you discussed in Section 1 Task 2 will help you to structure your ideas. Clarity also comes from a clear style.

Task 1

Read these three extracts.

1   Our enquiries have included interviews with three hundred potential customers, and we are satisfied that the product is entirely suitable for sale to the general public.

2   Interviews have been carried out with three hundred potential customers, and these enquiries have shown that the product is entirely suitable for sale to the general public.

3   I therefore got people to interview over three hundred potential customers as part of our enquiries, and I am sure that the product is exactly what the public want.

Which extract is the most formal? Why?
Which is the least formal? Why?
Which style is inappropriate for report writing? Why?

Some books on report writing suggest that the impersonal style in extract 2 is essential for formal reports. However, this form of writing is very difficult to control, and a document becomes difficult to read if it uses a lot of passive constructions like *An interview was carried out* or *An enquiry into what potential customers wanted was called for*. The style in the first extract should be suitable for most business reports.

4   The way we did it was...

In this section you will write a report on the way you carry out the next task.

Task 1

Try to do this task as quickly and efficiently as possible!

1   Organize yourselves in random groups of four.
2   Work together and arrange yourselves so that the average height in centimetres for the members of your group is the same as the average for the whole class.

Rules
- You can approach the task in any way you want.
- People can move from one group to another but the minimum size for a group is three people and the maximum is five.

Task 2

You are now going to write a report on how you and your group approached Task 1. Your aim is to
- describe what happened
- evaluate what you did
- provide recommendations for other students who will have to carry out the same task.

Use the following headings and notes to help you write your report.

Introduction
The aim of this section is to tell the reader what you are reporting on and why. Start with *We were asked to......*

Procedure
Tell the reader what you did. Use 'We' + the past tense where possible. Use numbers or linkers to make the sequence of events clear.

Discussion
Outline the advantages and disadvantages of what you did.

Recommendations
List ways of doing the task well. Use the formula *In order to do this task efficiently one must:*
    1...
    2...

Where possible use active constructions and simple vocabulary: for example, *We got into groups of four and read the task. We discussed it for a few minutes......*

Task 3

Exchange reports in small groups.

Which reports are particularly clear? Why?
Are there any reports that you especially agree or disagree with?
Why?

Task 4

If you want further practice in the area of report writing you might
want to consider these additional tasks.
- Write a report on an excursion or trip you have recently gone on.
  The main purpose of the report should be to make
  recommendations for future action.
- Write a report on the textbooks you are using to study English.
  Discuss your likes and dislikes and make suggestions for future
  improvements.

There is more work on report writing in *Writing – Advanced* in this
series.

Getting it right

1 Introduction

For most people effective writing is a result of planning, writing and rewriting. The first version is called a rough copy, and using a rough copy is a way of getting it right. When you are writing your rough copy it helps to leave every other line blank as this makes it easier to make changes and correct spelling.

The purpose of this unit is to sensitize you to areas you should be aware of when you look at your written work again.

2   A fair hand

Our attitude to a piece of written communication can be seriously affected by the handwriting so make sure your writing is easy to read.

Task 1

Each of these samples breaks one of the four major rules of English handwriting. Correct each sample and write out the appropriate rule under it. Discuss your answers with a partner before checking them on page 86.

1

There's a long way to go.

3

That film is on next week.

2

What a narrow view of life!

4   *It's a lovely colour*

Attention to simple rules of handwriting will make your work easier to read.

3   Introduction to punctuation

Punctuation is an important ingredient in writing. Poor punctuation creates a bad impression and can lose you marks if you are taking an exam.

Task 1

List the punctuation devices you know in English.
   For example: commas (, , ,).

Task 2

Work in a small group. Write down anything you know about the function of the devices on your list.

    For example: Apostrophes (' ') are used to show where letters have been left out of a contracted form, as in *can't, she's, I'd*, etc.

Now choose one device each and find out as much as you can about it. Use a reference source, such as *Practical English Usage* by Michael Swan, (Oxford University Press).

Task 3

Exchange information with the other students. Make notes under the following headings:

device	*function*	*example*
apostrophe	• to show where letters are left out of a contracted form	I'd.
	• to indicate possession	The girl's watch

4   Practice in punctuation

This section aims to give you practice which will illustrate some of the rules of punctuation.

Task 1

Which of the following words should start with a capital letter?

mango	*river*	*hope*
january	*the alps*	*the earth*
minute	*mountain*	*mars*
west	*elizabeth*	*chinese*
french	*tuesday*	*north africa*
professor	*winter*	*captain cook*
sea	*kentucky*	

Task 2

Rewrite each of the following with full stops and capital letters.

1   the french usually reserve the whole month of august for their holidays by the sea

2   australia's typical illegal immigrant is british and has set himself/herself up with a job and a false name britons are part of a group blamed for costing the taxpayer about £20 million a year

3   agony is socially unacceptable one is not supposed to weep when one is moderately presentable and thirty-two when one's wife has been dead for six months and everybody else has done grieving

Task 3

Rewrite the following sentences with capital letters, full stops and commas wherever they are needed.

1 mandy smith who claims she was the lover of bill wyman of the rolling stones when she was thirteen was yesterday questioned at scotland yard

2 the town was some shops the church the dispensary the methodist school my consulate

3 some white sugars are coloured brown during refining however so beware a sugar is only raw and unrefined if so indicated on the label

Task 4

Add quotation marks to these extracts.

1 Murderer, a woman shouted at the man in the passenger seat.

2 Yes. Jimmy looked at me. Quite. He paused slightly. The food was all right but the drinks . . .

3 A pint of lager, please. I said. I looked at his row of bottles. And a Bell's from that bottle, please.

Task 5

Some of the punctuation is missing from these passages. The places have been marked with a (∧). Insert the missing punctuation marks.

1 When the worlds most famous recluse, Howard Hughes, died in April 1976, on an aeroplane flying him from Acapulco to Houston for medical treatment the full horror of his descent into madness had still to be revealed. Yet ever since going into complete seclusion in 1950 he had been the subject of continual interest.

2 The Industrial Revolution is a long train of changes starting about 1760. It is not alone it forms one of a triad of revolutions of which the other two were the American Revolution that started in 1775 and the French Revolution that started in 1789. The fact is they were all social revolutions. The Industrial Revolution is simply the English way of making those social changes.

3 **Postmen deliver headache to DA**
   The District Attorney in Philadelphia is considering criminal charges against a local doctor after postal workers 500 miles away opened a consignment marked aerosol cans only to discover that it contained twelve human heads en route to a medical research centre in the Rockies.
   The traffic has been going on for fifteen years.
   The fact that the postal workers in Louisville, Kentucky, hastily closed the lid on the boxs contents and sent it on its way to its destination in

Denver Colorado is only one bizarre feature of the case. When Philadelphia police raided the office of Dr Martin Spector they found eight pairs of frozen ears prompting the city's Daily News to splash across yesterdays front page the memorable headline Ears found in probe on heads.

Dr Spector an ear nose and throat specialist who is not currently talking to reporters apparently told police that he had been sending similar items in plastic bags containing preservatives for fifteen years. Police have not yet established whether he trafficked in ears noses and throats for profit.

Dr Spector could be charged under an old Pennsylvania law known as 'abuse of corpse' whereby it is illegal to handle bodies in a way that would offend the deceased's family. A fine of up to $5,000 and two years imprisonment is possible.

The whole case gives me a headache the District Attorney Mr Ron Castille is reported to have said.

5　Is this what you mean?

Reread what you write! Careless word order or an unintentional spelling mistake can give your work a new meaning!

Task 1

These extracts suffer from careless word order. Guess what the writer intended to say and produce a corrected version.

1　You will find some wine you can take in the fridge.

2　No child should be employed on any weekday when the school is not open for a longer period than four hours.

3　He only made one visit which aroused the interest of the police.

4　He took a letter with an angry gesture from the file, and threw it on the counter.

5　It is about time your workmen came back to fill the hole because we are fed up of having it in the street, it is a big attraction and we are getting children by the dozen.

Task 2

The following extracts are taken from newspapers and magazines. The editor has failed to find mistakes that make the extracts unintentionally funny. Can you find the mistakes?

1　Perhaps the only disappointment of the championships from the British point of view was the defeat of Ade Mafe in the 200 metres at the hands of that good American sprinter Mel Lattany. It was in this Cosford stadium this time last year that Ade first hit the headlines by

eating Lattany but yesterday he was not ready for another big race
so soon after his silver medal performance in the world indoor games
in Paris last week.   *The Observer*

2 Intelligent and
Enthusiastic
Person Wanted
to organise this department.
Will entail baking,
buying
and serving customers   *Worthing Gazette & Herald*

3 It costs at least $1500 per competitor at either the Commonwealth
or Olympic Games, or at world titles. It does not take an accountant
to figure out that a 10-man Australian team overseas costs at least
$150,000.   *The Australian*

4 8.00 Bodymatters
In the first of eight new programmes the subject is teeth — they are
built to last a lifetime, yet every year British dentists put in 34 million
fillings and take ouch 11 million teeth.   *The Scotsman*

5 Found guilty of smuggling drugs into southern China, Mr Zheng
Jianwei, a Hong Kong businessman has been sentenced to death,
suspended for two years.   *The Guardian*

6   Practice in correcting drafts

The procedure you use when you reread a final draft is very personal
but it is important to be systematic. We need to check
* the order in which information is presented (Is it clear, logical and
  effective?)
* the layout
* spelling
* punctuation
* handwriting
* word order
* choice of words
* grammar (especially the form and choice of tenses)

When you have checked all these, you should go through the text
again and look for omissions. Is there any other information which
you need to include? Is there any unnecessary repetition? As this
excerpt from an advertisement for a computer printer indicates, our
aim should be to say what we want to say as clearly and as simply as
possible.

Finally, it is very important that you try and use expressions that are
appropriate.

Fifteen ways ~~and means~~
to ~~substantially~~
sharpen up your ~~writing of~~
~~a~~ business letters.

Task 1

Look at these examples of letters written by foreign students during EFL exams. The places where the work can be improved have been underlined. Rewrite the letters after you have discussed them in pairs or small groups. You can change the order of the paragraphs if you want to. Make sure you correct all the spelling and punctuation mistakes.

Letter 1

11, Burley Road
Parkstone
Poole
Dorset
BH12 ⟨x⟩ 3DA
14th March 1985

Grand Hotel
Broad Street
Bristol

Dear Sir or Madam
I stayed in your Hotel last week. I was there from the 4th of March until the 12th of March 1985. I had room 216 in the second floor. I think I forgot my pair of sportshoes and my washing things. My sportshoes are white and the number is 37. My washing things are in a blue bag.
I will be grateful if you will be able to send these to me. So soon as possible please.
I enclosing the postage.
I'm looking forward to meeting you in the near future.

Yours Faithfully
R. Bergesen

Letter 2

Virgin Records Ltd,
Marble Arch,
London W1.

Magdalena Percy,
9 Oak Gardens,
London W2.
11 December 1984

Dear Sirs,
With reference to your famous reputation, I bought a radio-cassette three days ago in your shop.
Therefore, it is not working properly. Every time I want to use it, I cannot get a loud and nice sound from my radio-cassette. I thought it might be the dusty, so I cleaned the heads of the radio-cassette with cotton and spirit. But it still does not work. I think there is a mechanical deffect, because I always take care of my things and it is the first time this happens.
I would like to know if you could repaired it, it is a very nicer piece of technologie. i have still my receipt of one year garantee. Also, I have enclosed the photocopie of that receipt and the radio-cassette which you will find it with the letter.
Looking forward to hear from you again.
Yours faithfully,
Marie-Noel Lefayre

Task 2

Try to improve the two passages below written by foreign students during an exam. Start by identifying all the spelling, grammar, vocabulary and punctuation errors.

When you have finished go through the passages again and see if you can make them easier to read by changing the order of some of the sentences or adding some linkers and sequencers.
Write out your own versions of the passages. Discuss them in small groups.

Passage 1

Two years ago it was the worst day of my life. I woke up one hour late I didn't heard the bells of the church. I would have never known if they had forgotten to ring the bells or if I had slept too deeply. I live near the church so i wake up when the bells ring at seven o'clock.

During that night I had a terrible nightmare, I dreamt that my grandmother was fought by two gansters in London.

In the morning it was raining and very cold I tried to make my coffee but the water had frozen during the night so I didn't take my breakfast. The postman brought two letters. One was the bill of my insurance of my car and the other was a very bad news: the depth of a closed friend. then I was so depressed that I missed my bus to go to work. Wen I arrived at the factory my boss told me I could find an another job because the factory will brake down in one month.

I didn't know what to do.

Passage 2

My ealiest memories are about 'Shichigosan' when I was three years old. In Japan, on november 15th, mostly children wear special tradintional dress, for example, 'kimono' for girls and 'hakama' for boys. It is very special selemony. We call this 'Shichigosan'. Parents wish their children will be fine. When I was three years old, I wore dress like white wedding dress, not kimono, which my mother made. I liked this dress very much. I showed my dress to my grandmother and neighbour. Then my parents and I went to shrine to wish something. when we got there, I saw many children wore kimono (except me) I was very surprised. I was sad, then I cried loudly. I didn't know why I cried. Then I wanted to wear kimono. I told my mother 'I don't want to wear dress. I want to wear kimono!' I worried my parents very much. These are my earliest memories.

KEY

UNIT 2

5 Choosing your words carefully
Task 1
1 Extract **A** is about industrial relations. Extract **B** is about international understanding.

UNIT 3

3 Telling a story
Task 2
A poor man was passing through Ak-Sehir with only a piece of dry bread between himself and starvation. As he passed by an eating-house, he saw some very appetizing meatballs frying in a pan over the charcoal fire, and carried away by the delicious smell, he held his piece of dry bread over the pan in the hope of capturing some of it. Then he ate his bread, which seemed to taste better. The restaurant owner, however, had seen what was going on, and seizing the man by the scruff of the neck, dragged him off to see the cadi, (a judge), who at this time happened to be Nasreddin Hodja, and demanded that he be compelled to pay the price of the pan of meatballs.
The Hodja listened attentively, then drew two coins from his pocket. 'Come here a minute,' he said to the restaurant owner. The latter obeyed, and the Hodja enclosed the coins in his fist and rattled them in the man's ear. 'What is the meaning of this?' said the restaurant owner. 'I have just paid you your damages,' said the Hodja. 'The sound of money is fair payment for the smell of food.'

Task 3
1 when I locked my grandma in the cupboard
2 was
3 came
4 had gone
5 just shut it
6 she started to shout
7 she would wait there
8 sat thinking
9 let my grandma out of the cupboard
10 came in

UNIT 4

3 Headings can help
Task 1
The three missing headings in the original advertisement are:
Endless creative opportunities
Play back directly through any TV
Light and portable

UNIT 5

1 Introduction
Task 1
1 reply; decide who the letter is from.
2 it will find its way to the right person.
3 people find the letter you are replying to.
4 will make sure they get your name right.
5 the subject of the letter.
6 tell the reader why you are writing.

Task 2
Basic rules for letters and titles can be found in *Practical English Usage* by Michael Swan (OUP).

6 'Yours faithfully' is the most formal of these and is usually only used when we don't know the name of the person we are writing to.
'Yours sincerely' and 'Yours truly' are often used in business letters.
'Yours ever' is a less formal way of closing a business or personal letter than 'Yours sincerely'.
'Yours' is an informal way of closing a letter to someone you know well.
'Love' is used for friendly personal letters.

3 Get a feel for style
Task 3

number	function
1	greeting
2	giving a reason for writing (stating the problem)
3 and 4	explaining the problem
5	suggesting a solution (request for action)
6	threat of future action if nothing is done
7	closing

UNIT 6

2   Introducing the issue
Task 1

Extract	Topic	How it is introduced
2	Debt problem of the Third World	Facts and figures to support argument
3	Problems of service workers	Direct appeal to reader
4	Discussion of social security	Series of questions to involve reader in argument
5	Effect of drunken drivers	A major statistic to underline how unfair situation is

3   Presenting your arguments
Task 1
1   But why should this situation continue?
2   But what about Britain?

Task 2
If... By... because... But... What...
yet... the reason... Since... After all

4   Coming to a conclusion
Task 1
The original ordering for the text was:
2, 4, 5, 1, 6, 3

UNIT 7

1   Introduction
Task 1
Extract 1   builder's publicity
Extract 2   a report
Extract 3   a letter

3   Creating a mood
Task 1
gold... blue... purples and pinks... red...
turquoise and aquamarines... emerald green...

Task 2
The Old Alley
Soaked papers cling to *aged* stone,
Dustbin lids rock to and fro in the *light* wind,
Milk cartons, beer bottles and newspapers
Squeeze through holed, rusty and *overloaded* bins.
Broken drainpipes hang from *decaying* and
    depressing walls,
Thieving rats raid *abandoned* houses.
A *malodorous* smell reeks from open drains,
Shattered windows reveal *dark* and musty places
    behind.
Shadows hang dolefully on *cracked* brick,
The echoes of children playing bounces back off
Each alley wall.

A *homeless* dog limps in the gutter,
Sniffing at the drains — whining for food.
(From a poem by Richard Partridge.)

UNIT 9

2   How did it happen?
Task 1
The following expressions can be used, (others may also be acceptable):

1   because... as a result... therefore...
2   while... Although...

Connectors like these are very important in reports. Make sure you know how the past continuous tense works.

UNIT 10

2   A fair hand
Task 1
The four major rules of English handwriting are:
1   Write on the line
2   Make sure the letters (except for capitals) are the same size
3   Make sure the slope is consistent
4   Make sure the space between letters is even

6   Practice in correcting drafts
Task 1
These are suggestions for improved versions of what the students wrote. Other versions may be acceptable.

Letter 1

> 11, Burley Road
> Parkstone
> Poole
> Dorset BH12 3DA
>
> 14th March 1985

Grand Hotel
Broad Street
Bristol

Dear Sir or Madam

I stayed in your Hotel last week. I was there from the 4th of March until the 12th of March 1985. I stayed in room 216 on the second floor.

I think I forgot my pair of trainers and my washing things. My trainers are white and size 37. My washing things are in a blue bag.

I would be grateful if you could send these to me as soon as possible.

I am enclosing the postage.

Looking forward to hearing from you in the near future.

Yours faithfully

Letter 2

Magdalena Percy,
9 Oak Gardens,
London W2.

Virgin Records Ltd.,   11 December 1984
Marble Arch,
London W1.

Dear Sirs,

Three days ago, I bought a radio-cassette in your shop because of your famous reputation.

However, it is not working properly. Every time I want to use it, I cannot get a decent sound. I thought it might be dust, so I cleaned the heads of the radio-cassette with cotton and spirit. But, it still does not work. I think there is a mechanical defect, because I always take care of my things and it is the first time this has happened to me.

I would like to know if you could repair it. It is a very nice piece of technology. I still have my receipt and one year guarantee. I am enclosing a photocopy of that receipt and the radio-cassette.

Looking forward to hearing from you.

Yours faithfully,

Task 2

These are suggestions for improved versions of what the students wrote. Other versions may be acceptable.

Passage 1

The worst day of my life was two years ago. I woke up one hour late because I didn't hear the church bells. I live near the church so I usually wake up when the bells ring at seven o'clock. However, I will never know if the vicar forgot to ring the bells or if I had slept too deeply. During the night I'd had a terrible nightmare. I dreamt that my grandmother was attacked by two gangsters in London.

In the morning it was raining and very cold. I tried to make my coffee but the water had frozen during the night so I didn't get any breakfast. The postman brought two letters. One was the bill for my car insurance and the other was very bad news: the death of a close friend. As a result, I was so depressed that I missed my bus to work. When I arrived at the factory my boss told me I could find another job because the factory would be closing down in a month.

I didn't know what to do.

Passage 2

My earliest memories are about 'Shichigosan' when I was three years old. 'Shichigosan' is a special ceremony in Japan. It takes place on November 15th. Most children wear special traditional dress, 'kimono' for girls and 'hakama' for boys, and parents go to a shrine to wish their children well. When I was three years old, I wore a dress which my mother made. It was like a white wedding dress. I liked the dress very much and showed it to my grandmother and neighbour. Then my parents and I went to the shrine to make a wish. When we got there, I saw that except for me, all the girls were wearing kimonos. I was very surprised and sad and then I began to cry loudly. I told my mother 'I don't want to wear a dress. I want to wear a kimono!' I don't know why I cried but this worried my parents very much. These are my earliest memories.